Stamp in Color

Techniques for
Enhancing Your Artwork

DAVE BRETHAUER

Martingale
& COMPANY

Bothell, Washington

MISSION
STATEMENT

We are dedicated to providing quality products and service by working together to inspire creativity and to enrich the lives we touch.

Credits

President . . . . Nancy J. Martin
CEO . . . . Daniel J. Martin
Publisher . . . . Jane Hamada
Editorial Director . . . . Mary V. Green
Design and Production Manager . . . . Stan Green
Editorial Product Manager . . . . Tina Cook
Technical Editor . . . . Candie Frankel
Copy Editor . . . . Miriam Bulmer
Illustrator . . . . Laurel Strand
Photographer . . . . Brent Kane
Cover and Text Designer . . . . Rohani Design

Stamp in Color: Techniques for Enhancing Your Artwork
© 2000 by Dave Brethauer

Martingale & Company
PO Box 118
Bothell, WA 98041-0118 USA
www.martingale-pub.com

Printed in the United States of America
05 04 03 02 01 00   6 5 4 3 2 1

Library of Congress Cataloging-in-Publication Data

Brethauer, Dave,
    Stamp in color : techniques for enhancing your artwork / Dave Brethauer.
        p. cm.
    ISBN 1-56477-329-9
        1. Greeting cards. 2. Rubber stamp printing. 3. Colored pencil
    drawing—Technique. 4. Watercolor painting—Technique. I. Title.

TT872 .B74 2000
761—dc21   00-058732

Contents

How to Use This Book ~ 4

Working with Watercolors ~ 5

    Tools and Materials ~ 5
    Easy Watercolor Techniques ~ 9

Working with Colored Pencils ~ 13

    Tools and Materials ~ 14
    Easy Colored Pencil Techniques ~ 15

Assembling the Cards ~ 18

    Working with Paper ~ 18
    Stamping and Embossing ~ 22
    Using a Computer and Printer ~ 24

Spring ~ 26

    Spring Palette of Colors ~ 27
    Wedding Invitation ~ 28
    Bridal Shower Invitation ~ 32
    Bouquet Card ~ 34
    Framed Charm Card ~ 36
    Butterfly Card ~ 38
    Baby Announcement ~ 40
    Baby Carriage Card ~ 42
    Flower Patch Card ~ 44

Summer ~ 46

    Summer Palette of Colors ~ 47
    House on a Hill Card ~ 48
    Swirly Butterfly Card ~ 50
    Bunny Card ~ 52
    Birthday Cake Card ~ 54
    Potted Flower Card ~ 56

    Flower Wreath Card ~ 58
    Birthday Presents Card ~ 58
    Five-Petaled Flower Card ~ 62

Autumn ~ 66

    Autumn Palette of Colors ~ 67
    Teacup Quattro Card ~ 68
    Cooper's First Sunrise Card ~ 70
    Autumn Tree Card ~ 72
    Wardrobe Card ~ 74
    Pumpkin Card ~ 76

Winter ~ 78

    Winter Palette of Colors ~ 79
    Christmas Tree Card ~ 80
    Christmas Present Card ~ 82
    Snowman Gift Tag ~ 84
    Star Over Neighborhood Card ~ 86
    Four Snowmen and Star Card ~ 88
    Snowman and Star Card ~ 90
    Single Snowman Card ~ 92

Source Guide ~ 94

About the Author ~ 95

How to Use This Book

It is the intent of this book to provide clear, detailed, and fun instruction on coloring techniques for beginning rubber stampers. The most wonderful thing about rubber stamping is that it isn't hard. There are a few tricks you can learn, however, to make your projects more beautiful and professional looking. Combining these basic watercolor and colored pencil techniques with rubber stamping will turn your handmade greeting cards into miniature works of art.

The first few chapters provide an introduction to the tools and materials you will be using. Color photos will help you learn the basics, step by step, at your own pace. Refer to these pages when you want to choose a watercolor paper, create a wash, or blend pencil colors. There's also a brief section on card-making techniques.

The remainder of the book is devoted to individual projects to try throughout the year, season by season. I've chosen designs that are simple and elegant, a good rule to adhere to in card making. For each season—spring, summer, autumn, and winter—there is a suggested palette of colors and five to eight projects in a variety of techniques. The techniques become more involved as the book goes on, but all are accessible for beginning students. With this book, I hope to share with a wider audience the techniques I have demonstrated in my workshops as well as the valuable design and color insights I have gained from other instructors and stylists over my years of card making.

Working with Watercolors

There is nothing quite like the look of watercolor. A perfect wash of color across a sky or a smooth blend over the surface of a leaf can make a person do a double take. Even the word watercolor is romantic.

Watercolor techniques can be elusive. They involve planning and timing but also stepping back and letting the paint do more or less its own thing. It is hard to control these watery paints, but often you don't want to—their unpredictable nature is also their allure. In this section, you will learn about the tools, materials, and techniques required to start making your own watercolor magic.

TOOLS AND MATERIALS

Brushes

Despite the wide variety of brushes available, choosing the right one for your project is relatively easy, once you know the basics. Brushes come in different types, shapes, and sizes. Which brush you choose depends on the size of your project and the techniques you want to use when painting.

Brush Types

Paintbrushes are made either with synthetic fibers, such as nylon, or with natural fibers, such as animal hairs. Synthetic brushes are the less

expensive of the two, and they do perform well, especially for small projects. However, you may find you prefer a natural-fiber brush. Natural bristles are soft and flexible. They lay down the paint smoothly and they also seem to hold more paint, letting you color larger areas before reloading.

Brush Shapes

Paintbrushes are designed in different shapes for different jobs. Round brushes are the most effective for painting small detailed areas. Flat brushes are excellent for filling in large areas with a wash of color. The shape of the brush can also affect how much paint can be loaded into the bristles.

Brush Sizes

Keep in mind the area you will be painting when choosing a paintbrush size. For card-size projects, I recommend a No. 4 or No. 6 round brush. These sizes will allow you to paint small areas in a stamped image accurately. For more expansive areas, you may find a larger round brush more efficient, particularly if you are a beginner. Occasionally I will use a 1" flat brush to surround a stamped image with color. In watercolor painting, the faster you paint an area, the more even the color will appear when dry.

Brush Care

Avoid letting your brushes stand in a cup of water for extended periods of time. When you finish painting, rinse your brush in clear water, pull the bristles to a point, and lay the brush flat to dry. Stand dry brushes upright in a container so the bristles aren't pressing against anything.

Watercolor Paper

Watercolor paper is thick and richly textured. The paint finds its way into the thousands of dimples across the paper surface in such a way that both the paper and the color appear richer and more intense. Watercolor paper can be purchased in blocks, in tablets, or as individual sheets.

Watercolor Blocks

A watercolor block is a stack of watercolor papers glued together on all four sides. You stamp and paint on the top sheet while it is still attached. The paint will not leak through to the next sheet, and the glued sides keep the paper flat so that you don't need to worry about curling as you add

The sealed edges of a watercolor block help the paper remain flat during painting.

water to the surface. When your finished work is dry, simply insert a brush handle or butter knife into the small unglued opening on the block to peel off the top layer.

Watercolor Tablets and Sheets

Sheets of watercolor paper can be purchased in tablet form or individually. You can choose either machine-made or handmade papers. Since the edges are not fixed in place, as they are in a block, it is possible for some curling to occur during painting. On small projects this curling tends to be minimal, but if you are painting a large area with copious amounts of paint and water you may want to stretch your sheet first. Soak the sheet in room-temperature water for a few minutes, then lay it out on a smooth, flat work surface. Soak up the excess water with a sponge and then smooth out the paper with your hand. Secure all four edges with tape or pushpins (depending on your work surface) so that the sheet will remain flat as it dries. Once the sheet is dry, you can begin working on it without having the edges curl on you.

Handmade (top) and machine-made sheets.

Paper Weights and Surfaces

Examine a sheet of watercolor paper and you will see that it is made to absorb a lot of liquid. I use 140-lb. paper, a common machine-made paper weight, for most of my projects. A paper's weight refers to the density of its fibers; the heavier the weight, the thicker the paper. Keep in mind, though, that weight is not always an accurate indicator of a handmade paper's thickness because of the variations inherent in any given sheet.

A paper's surface feel depends on whether it was manufactured using a hot-press method (for a smooth surface) or a cold-press method (for a textured surface). Smooth hot-press watercolor papers are used for illustration techniques such as pen-and-ink drawings that are then colored with watercolor. For coloring in stamped images, I prefer the texture of cold-press papers. The microscopic jags and valleys on the surface give the paper some tooth so that the paint has something to hold onto. Textured paper seems to make the painting process more forgiving. For a rougher texture yet, you can experiment with handmade watercolor papers.

Watercolor Paints

The gorgeous tones and shading associated with watercolors are the result of complex paint pigments. So many different shades are available that the selection may at first seem overwhelming. As a beginner you will need only a few basic colors, but once you acquire a feel for what shades work well together you may find yourself desiring a "greener" blue or a red with more orange in it. As you progress, you will discover which colors you are naturally drawn to and also how to mix, blend, and create washes to achieve a virtually endless range of shades.

Choosing Your Paints

Watercolor pigment is sold in dry solid blocks or wet in tubes. Dry paints can be challenging to work with. They need to be wetted quite often, and trying to lift up paint that is not sufficiently moist can be hard on your paintbrush.

Still, dry pigments are convenient and are often preferable for travel because of their compact, portable nature.

The paint pigment sold in tubes is concentrated and must be extended with water in order to be usable. Although tube watercolors may seem intimidating at first, I recommend them because they blend easily and the colors are fabulous. To use the paint, simply squeeze a small amount onto a palette (I use a dinner plate) and mix in a few drops of water using your paintbrush. The more water you add, the paler the color. Several different colors can be deposited around the edge of the plate, with plenty of room left in the middle for mixing. This approach can become messy and requires planning to avoid waste. Paint that has dried on the plate can be reconstituted, but the results are unpredictable and the paint may not mix evenly.

Understanding Paint Colors

Choosing and mixing the colors you will use in your projects is sometimes more fun than the painting itself. A simple color chart that you paint yourself will help you develop your own sense of what combinations work well.

A key concept to remember is that there is no "true" red, "true" blue, or "true" yellow with watercolor paints. The color red, for instance, might be cadmium red, which is an orange-red, or alizarin crimson, a violet-red. Understanding that the red you use may be more orange or more violet will allow you to create a mix that produces precisely the shade you are looking for. For example, in some projects you may want a muted orange and in others you may want a brilliant orange. Knowing how to obtain these shades is easy once you understand the color bias already present in the paints.

Add a squirt of tube paint to the palette and then add water off to the side of the squirt of paint. To make the color paler, add water. To make the color stronger, pull in more paint. Watercolor palettes come in a variety of shapes and sizes as shown below.

When mixing analogous hues, choose colors that are close to one another on the color wheel for a bright shade and hues that are farther apart for a muted shade. Here, cadmium red + cadmium yellow = brilliant orange, while alizarin crimson + lemon yellow = muted orange.

EASY WATERCOLOR TECHNIQUES

Water is obviously an element in all watercolor techniques. If you're just getting acquainted with watercolors, begin by brushing the surface of the paper liberally with plain water. This prewetting ensures that the paint will achieve full, smooth, even coverage and that it won't dry prematurely, leaving behind paint lines or brush marks. Over time, as you develop your skills and learn how to paint quickly, prewetting will become optional and you can just jump right into a project.

Water also helps you control the color saturation. For lighter, softer, more transparent color, use more water. For stronger, more intense color, use less water and more paint. This principle becomes especially relevant when you begin blending colors on paper. C-23

The same color diluted with light, moderate, and generous amounts of water.

The amount of water in a paint mixture also affects how it interacts with other paint mixtures. If one mix has more water than another, the more diluted mix will push the less diluted color out of the way.

A mixture with more water will push its way into a neighboring color. The results are wonderfully unpredictable.

Tip *Putting a drop of paint into a wet area is a fun, unpredictable technique. Once dry, the color will be strongest where it was initially deposited and show a gradual fade from this spot.*

Washes

A wash—the technique most often associated with watercolor—is a perfect, flowing gradation of color across an area. A wash may involve only one color that fades from dark to light, or it may feature a combination of colors—for example, green into blue into purple. The ability of this fluid medium to gradually shift through the colors of the spectrum is amazing.

Painting a Watercolor Wash

1. Determine the area you want the wash to fill. Prewet this area by brushing it with plain water. The surface should be slightly wet, so that you can see a sheen.

2. Squeeze some paint onto your palette, enough to fill the wash area (you don't want to run out of paint midway). Mix the paint with your brush, adding a little water to make it spreadable.

3. Touch a corner of the prewetted area with the loaded brush. You will observe the paint spreading into the wet area on its own.

4. Slowly brush the paint across the prewetted area, keeping the tip of the brush on the paper as much as possible. To avoid dried paint lines, work into the paint edge while it is still wet.

5. When your brush runs out of paint, pull it to the edge of the wet area and lift it off the paper. (Removing the brush in the middle will create a noticeable drop of color at that spot.) Reload the brush with paint and continue, starting inside the painted area and working toward your endpoint.

6. A successful wash will show a gradual change of color across the area. The color may fade out or randomly brighten and soften.

Tip *The colors in a wash lighten as they dry. If your wash looks a little stronger or darker when wet than you intended, then you're doing it correctly.*

Blending

Blending is a watercolor skill that yields spectacular results, simultaneously adding color interest and depth. The goal is to lay down two or more colors and then mix them together so that they create new in-between colors that flow seamlessly, one into another.

Painting the initial color areas is relatively easy, but creating a flawless blend takes practice. It is essential to use enough liquid, so that the area connecting two colors does not stand out. Start with similar paint-to-water ratios for each color. As your blending skills increase, you can try varying the ratios for more interesting and unexpected results. A more watery mixture, remember, will push an adjacent color out of the way.

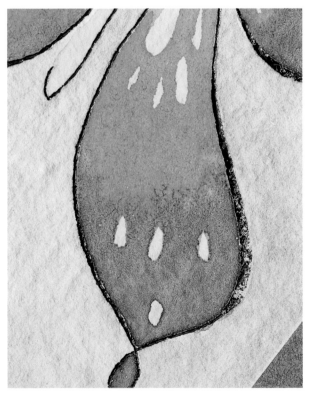

Skillful blending lends drama to this butterfly wing.

Tip *For more control over the color mix, rinse the brush between each color. If the colors aren't blending at all, then the paint is drying out too quickly. Try working faster, or use more paint on your brush.*

Blending Watercolors

1. Select the colors you want to blend. Squeeze equal amounts of each onto your palette, and add equal amounts of water to each for a spreadable consistency.
2. Define the area you will paint by prewetting the area with plain water.
3. Visually divide the area into sections, one for each color. Starting at one corner, begin applying the lightest color to the first of the sections.

4. Dip your brush, without rinsing, into the second color on your palette. Begin painting the second section. Drag this color a little bit into the first section's color to encourage their mixing.

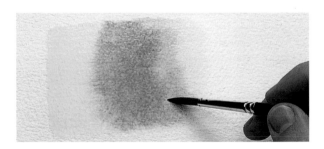

5. Dip your brush, again without rinsing, into the third color and paint the third section. Drag the second and third colors together, keeping the brush on the paper.

Tip *Blending analogous colors (colors that are next to each other on the color wheel) is easier than blending complementary colors (colors that are opposite one another on the color wheel). For a smooth analogous*

blend, try cadmium yellow, a mix of cadmium yellow and cadmium red, and cadmium red.

Layering Color

Another aspect of watercolor pigments is their transparency/opacity. There are four basic gradations—transparent, semitransparent, semiopaque, and opaque—with some hues being more "see-through" than others. Layering one of the more transparent colors over a base coat can produce exciting new colors. For instance, when you paint Windsor blue over a dry underlayer of lemon yellow, the result is a complex shade of blue with rich yellow undertones. Unlike mixing, in which two hues are combined to make a third hue (for example, yellow + blue = green), layering is a way of "influencing" a color

Layered colors.

by allowing another color to show through it. The effect is subtle and mysterious.

Layering Watercolors

1. Paint the selected area in a solid color, such as cadmium yellow. Since you want a solid underlayer, no prewetting is required.
2. Let the paint dry completely, preferably overnight.
3. Paint a wash of cadmium red over the cadmium yellow. Try to make one end a strong red and slowly fade out the color as you move across. (See "Painting a Watercolor Wash," page 10.)

Note how the underpainted and plain cadmium reds differ. Also note how the yellow shows up more and more as the cadmium red wash fades.

Erasing Mistakes

I have always felt that there's no such thing as a mistake when you paint a project. If, however, you feel the need to remove a stray brushstroke or two, here's a technique you can use. It's best to act quickly, while the paint is still wet.

Removing Watercolor Paint

1. Rinse your brush and squeeze out the excess water.
2. Touch your brush to the stray mark and soak up the paint. Repeat steps 1 and 2 as needed.

3. If the brush is not successful in picking up any of the color, the paint has probably dried. Carefully rewet the area with plain water, then repeat steps 1 and 2.

Working with Colored Pencils

Colored pencils are an incredible medium. They come in a spectacular array of colors and are capable of such flawless blending that people are often amazed to discover that colored pencils were used. Coloring with pencils is slow going compared to watercolors, but it affords greater control. There's no liquid moving where you don't want it to, which minimizes the guesswork. Colored pencils are convenient to use, easy to take along when you travel, and practically maintenance-free. A good pencil sharpener is all you'll need.

TOOLS AND MATERIALS

Paper

You can use just about any type of paper for colored pencil work as long as it has "tooth"—microscopic jags and valleys on the surface that the colored pencil can grab onto. The possibilities include card stock, handmade papers, and ordinary white drawing paper. Avoid glossy, coated papers—your pencil will merely glide across the surface. You can use heavily textured papers, but you'll need to press harder when coloring so as to slightly flatten the surface.

Wax-Based Colored Pencils

The colored pencils I recommend for rubber stamp projects have soft, wax-based pigments. If you think back to your school days, you may remember coloring with pencils that had very hard leads. This type is excellent for drawing but less effective for coloring. Wax-based pencils, in contrast, are soft and creamy. They provide smooth, opaque coverage, which means you can use them on colored papers as well as white backgrounds. They lend themselves to blending and layering, letting you create new shades as you color.

Pencil Sharpeners

You'll be using your pencil sharpener often, so choose it with care. Handheld sharpeners are effective but can be hard on your hands with frequent use. If you opt for an electric sharpener, choose a heavy-duty model that stops automatically once the pencil is sharpened. Models that vibrate excessively tend to crack the soft, wax-based lead inside the pencil shaft. Don't bother sharpening your pencils to a needle point; the tips will break off as soon as they are pushed onto the paper.

EASY COLORED PENCIL TECHNIQUES

The underlying beauty of colored pencil techniques is that they give an artist time to plan. If watercolors offer serendipity and surprise, colored pencils offer just the opposite: control. You don't need to rush with colored pencils. If a color doesn't seem right, you can add a little more of what's needed and blend it out over and over again, even days after you started. Once you've learned the basics of fading and blending, these relaxing techniques will give you a chance for meditation and will carry you back to your grade school days when your assignment was to color something in.

Fading

You probably learned a long time ago that if you didn't have a pink pencil, you could color lightly with a red pencil to create a "pink" substitute. When you color lightly, depositing only a small amount of pigment onto the paper, you achieve light saturation. When you press hard and really work the pencil into the paper surface—a technique called "burnishing"—you achieve heavy saturation.

You can achieve both heavy and light saturation with the same pencil.

It takes some practice to make a fade with no noticeable drops in color.

If there is an abrupt jump, use small circle strokes with medium pressure to smooth out the fade.

Of course, there are many degrees of saturation in between heavy burnishing and the very palest trace of color. These variations in saturation allow you to suggest areas of relative shadow and light in your work. A gradual movement from a darker to a lighter area is called a "fade." Fading is a valuable technique to learn in and of itself, and it is also the preliminary step in another technique, blending.

Colored Pencil Fading

1. Determine the area you want the fade to cover. Visualize the fade as a gradual, even shift of color across this area, and determine where the dark, medium, and light tones will fall. I tend to shade from left to right. Decide which direction will work for you and turn the paper accordingly.
2. Starting at the "dark" side, burnish the color into the paper using up-and-down strokes. Continue these up-and-down strokes and at the same time slowly move the pencil to the right, gradually letting up on the pressure to lighten the color. Strive for a smooth, gradual lightening, with no abrupt changes in color.
3. As you near the end of the area, use the lightest touch yet. To end the fade, barely touch the pencil to the paper so only a hint of pigment is applied. The fade should neither end too soon nor extend beyond the designated area.
4. Evaluate the fade. To smooth out jumps in color, make small circle strokes (about ⅛" diameter) in areas that need darkening.

Blending

Once you are familiar with saturation and fading, blending is the next technique you should develop. As in watercolor blending, two colors are laid down and then "mixed" together to create new in-between colors. With colored pencils, the soft, waxy pigments are actually crushed together, creating new colors without the addition of any liquids. The secret is heavy burnishing, so don't be afraid to press hard. When blending is done properly, it becomes hard to tell where one color stops and the next one starts.

A blend of three colors—poppy red, yellowed orange, and canary yellow. The canary yellow overlapped the yellowed orange, which overlapped poppy red. Canary yellow was used to blend them all together.

Use heavy pressure to achieve smooth, even blends of color.

Colored Pencil Blending

1. Pick two analogous colors (colors that are adjacent on the color wheel), such as chartreuse and canary yellow.
2. Use the canary yellow pencil to draw a 1" x ¼" box.
3. Working from left to right, begin coloring inside the box with the canary yellow pencil. Start with heavy saturation and gradually fade out the color until it disappears about ¼" from the right edge.
4. Begin coloring in the box with the chartreuse pencil. This time, start with heavy saturation on the right and gradually fade out the color toward the left, until the chartreuse disappears about ¼" from the left edge. You will be overlapping some of the yellow area as you go.

5. If you did both fades correctly, you should have a solid yellow area, about ¼" wide, at the left edge and a solid chartreuse area, also ¼" wide, at the right edge. Leave these areas alone.

6. Using the canary yellow pencil (the lighter color), burnish the middle area from right to left (toward the lighter color). Push hard so that all the green and yellow pigment is mashed together.

7. Use circle strokes about ⅛" in diameter to blend the edges of the middle area into the side areas. Circle strokes will help make your blend appear smoother because they are harder for the eye to pick up than straight up-and-down strokes.

Tip *Always start your blends with the lighter color. Make sure the color fades out completely and gradually. Any big jumps in color will be difficult to blend out.*

Colored pencil blending takes a little practice, but once mastered it will add drama to your projects. Once you know how to blend two colors, you'll be ready to blend multiple colors across an area, such as in the Star Over Neighborhood card (page 86). Always remember to blend with the lightest color and to push hard to crush the pigments together.

Erasing Mistakes

As with my watercolor projects, I rarely acknowledge colored pencil mistakes! Usually you can simply color over an area that didn't turn out to your liking. Stray marks outside the coloring area are admittedly difficult, if not impossible, to remove. Soft gum erasers sometimes work, or you can try putting masking tape on the area and lifting off the pigment. But I think you'll find that with the slow, methodical, controlled pace of colored pencil work, you're less likely to go off course to begin with.

Assembling the Cards

WORKING WITH PAPER

One of the most exciting parts of card design for me is choosing the different papers I will use. A paper's color and texture help define the spirit of the card, as can be seen in the Five-Petaled Flower card (page 62) with its "bright" and "soft" variations. One of my signature techniques, shown in the Bunny card (page 52), is to layer several contrasting papers to create a frame or matte effect around the art-

work. I also like to work with vellum and find that its soft, sophisticated, "see-through" quality is perfect for wedding stationery (page 28). For the card itself, be sure to choose a paper stiff enough to support all the layers you will be adding to it. Generally, I recommend 80-lb. cover weight, also known as card stock. Card stock has a firm, hefty feel and resists warping, whereas lighter weight papers tend to be too flimsy for greeting cards.

For each of the projects in this book, I list the specific papers I used and their dimensions. To cut rectangular pieces of paper for your cards, use either a paper cutter or an X-Acto knife and a straightedge (be sure to place a cutting mat underneath). Cut the pieces as precisely as possible. An exception is the paper on which you will stamp and color, since you will be trimming it further as the card making proceeds.

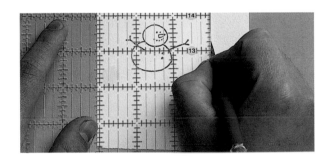

To cut irregular shapes, such as the bunnies for the Bunny card (page 52), lay the paper on the cutting mat, hold the knife blade at an angle, and draw the blade toward you. For smooth curves, rotate the paper as you move the knife. A sharp blade will cut easily; if you notice a drag, it's time for a blade replacement.

When a card is a unique size, such as the Teacup Quattro card (page 68), you will be cutting and folding the paper yourself to the precise dimensions required. When a design calls for a 4¼" x 5½" card, a standard size that fits an A2 envelope, you can use a purchased card or you can make your own. The window card, used in Cooper's First Sunrise (page 70), is another style that's easy to cut on your own if you don't want to use a purchased card.

Card-Making Supplies

No. 4 or No. 6 round paintbrush	Straightedge for cutting
Plate or palette	Cutting mat
Containers for rinse water	Eyelet setting tools
Pencil sharpener	⅛" hole punch
Heat gun	¼" hole punch
Computer and laser printer	Scissors
Bone folder	Ruler
Paper cutter (optional)	Pencil
X-Acto knife and extra blades	Double-coated tape

The following instructions describe how to make two standard-size cards from an 8½" x 11" sheet of card stock. The same approach can be applied to all the card projects in this book. In addition to your cutting tools, you will need a bone folder.

Making Standard Cards

1. Cut an 8½" x 11" sheet of card stock in half crosswise to make two 8½" x 5½" pieces.

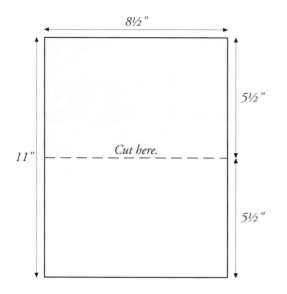

2. Lay one piece flat. Mark the midpoint of each 8½" edge, then line up a ruler to connect them.

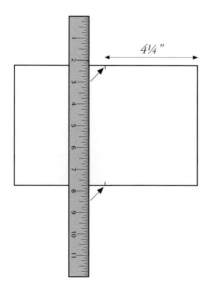

3. Drag the blunt tip of a bone folder along the edge of the ruler. Press firmly, compressing the paper fibers to make a narrow groove.

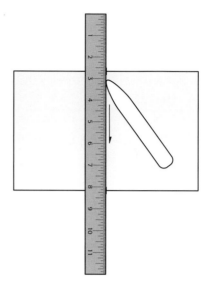

4. Fold the piece in half along the grooved line to make the card.

Repeat steps 2 through 4 to fold the remaining piece.

To mount the artwork and framing rectangles on a card, I use double-coated tape, which is less messy than glue. Generally, the artwork is centered on its framing rectangle, forming an even margin all around.

This piece is then mounted on the card, either centered, as in the Birthday Presents card (page 60), or positioned at the top of the card, as in the Birthday Cake card (page 54). Use the color photographs to guide you in the final assembly.

If you find you have difficulty centering the artwork on a "frame" rectangle, try starting with a slightly larger rectangle. Mount the artwork on the rectangle, but don't fuss about centering it perfectly. Then trim the frame to an even margin all around.

Some cards are accented with ribbon or metal eyelets. These accents can be purely decorative, or they can actually hold pieces of paper together, as in the Bouquet card (page 34). Eyelets are available in two sizes, $\frac{1}{8}$" and $\frac{3}{16}$", and a variety of colors. To install them, you will need a punch, a setter, a hammer, and a cutting mat. Punches have a round, hollow tip at the end that cuts a hole through the paper. Be sure to choose the correct punch size for your eyelet.

Punch, setter, hammer, and eyelets

Cut edge   *Trim line*

Installing an Eyelet

1. Layer the papers and lay them face up on a cutting mat. Set the tip of the punch on the desired spot. Hold the punch vertically and tap the end with a hammer to punch a hole through all the paper layers. The amount of pressure needed will depend on the thickness of the papers.

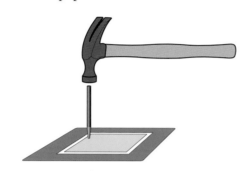

2. Insert the eyelet through the holes from front to back.

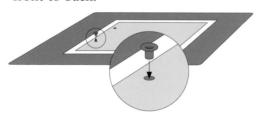

3. Turn the project over.

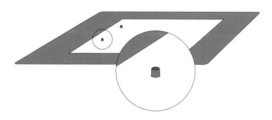

4. Insert the setting tool. To flange the eyelet, tap the setting tool with a hammer. A few short taps should be sufficient.

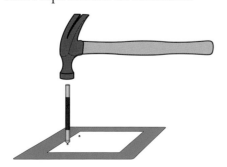

STAMPING AND EMBOSSING

When you stamp an image for coloring, it's essential to choose the appropriate ink. There are three basic choices. **Dye-based ink** dries quickly, making it a good choice for colored pencil work. You can start coloring almost immediately, without fear of smearing the ink. Dye-based inks are not waterproof, however, and will bleed if watercolors are applied. **Permanent ink** dries quickly on many papers and is waterproof, making it suitable for both colored pencils and watercolors. **Pigment-based ink** is used with heat-activated embossing powder to produce a raised impression of the stamped image. This ink dries slowly, giving the stamper a window of time in which to apply the embossing powder. On coated or glossy papers, such as vellum, the ink never dries completely and will smear if colored pencils are applied. Once pigment ink is embossed, however, both watercolors and colored pencils can be used.

Embossing works on almost any type of paper and is a boon to watercolor work because the small raised "walls" help contain the paint. Large, clear, open images look best because the powder spreads slightly as it melts. If your image is highly detailed, you can stamp with black ink and emboss with clear powder, or you can use detail embossing powder, an extra-fine powder specially formulated to bring out delicate lines. Clear powder gives you a beautiful raised embossed look but you will still be able to see the image clearly underneath. On the next page are some easy embossing instructions. You will need a heat gun.

Rubber Stamp Embossing

1. Stamp the image onto the paper using pigment-based ink.

2. Pour embossing powder onto the image, covering it completely.

3. Tap off the excess powder and funnel it back into the container for reuse. The powder that remains will stick to the stamped image.

4. Use a heat gun to blow hot air over the embossing powder for about 5 seconds, or until the powder melts.

5. In 10 to 15 seconds, the melted powder will cool and solidify, creating a permanent, slightly raised version of the stamped design.

USING A COMPUTER AND PRINTER

Combining computer-printed text with your rubber stamp artwork adds a professional quality to your cards and increases the variety of designs you can make. The computer is especially helpful in turning out multiple cards, such as wedding invitations or birth announcements. You will need to input your personal text and do some test printouts to verify how your text layout will fit in with the overall card design. As an example, in the Bouquet card (page 34), I began by printing *Congratulations* onto the center of a standard 8½" x 11" sheet of vellum. I next trimmed the vellum to the 5⅞" x 5⅞" size needed for the card, making sure that *Congratulations* remained centered. If a card design is small, such as a wedding invitation's reception and reply cards (page 28), you may be able to print several copies on one sheet and then trim them to the needed size.

Printing from a Computer

1. Open the word processing program.
2. Using the font you normally use for word processing (I like 12-point Times New Roman), enter your text line by line, flush with the left margin. For example:

Mr. and Mrs. Elliot Hill
Request the Honor of your Presence
at the marriage of their daughter
Pamela Christine
etc.

3. Once all the text has been entered, begin experimenting with the layout and design. You might center each line of text, use different fonts, adjust the point size, or vary the spacing between lines. For example:

Mr. and Mrs. Elliot Hill
Request the Honor of your Presence
at the marriage of their daughter
Pamela Christine

We are pleased
to announce the arrival
of

Emma Ruth Hill

born March 9, 2000
weighing 7 lb 4 oz
and measuring 20 in.

When you have a version you like, print it on ordinary paper.

4. Evaluate your printed text in terms of the card design. Does the font suit the mood of the card—i.e., formal, informal, sophisticated, juvenile? Is the text area too big or too small for the card, or will it fill the allotted area nicely? Would some words or phrases be better larger or smaller? Repeat steps 3 and 4 as needed to fine-tune the design.

5. Print your final version on the paper specified for the project. Trim the paper to the desired size and make one card start to finish. Make certain this prototype card is perfect before you print and trim the remaining pieces. Save the computer file so you can use it later for similar projects.

As with stamp-pad inks, some printers are better than others for card making. I recommend laser printers because the toner sticks to almost all papers and tends to give clean, crisp results. See if your laser printer has a port in the back so that you can feed the vellum or card stock through flat. There's less chance of a jam or warping this way.

Inkjet printers have the advantage of color printing, which can produce some interesting effects when coordinated with your rubber stamp artwork. Because inkjets use pigmented ink, they produce spectacular embossing effects. Just print your text, and as soon as the paper comes out of the printer, pour on the embossing powder and proceed as usual. Unfortunately, pigmented inkjet inks tend to bleed on vellum and other coated papers. You can get around this problem by printing your text onto regular paper and then having a photocopy shop copy it onto vellum for you.

Of course, rubber stamps can be used print cards as well. Literally hundreds of *Thank You* and *Happy Birthday* stamps are available. Or you can try piecing words together using alphabet sets. The individual letters are tricky to line up straight, so expect a playful look. You can also have a stamp professionally cut for a birth announcement or a party invitation; it makes a nice keepsake of the event.

Spring

Early spring has a gentle, diluted palette. Early-morning frosts soften the green grass, pale yellow crocuses blanket the garden, and the cool blue sky is just beginning to shine through after months of clouds. Spring uses an array of these gentle colors to quietly announce its arrival. These pastel shades can be used as a neutral background for elegant invitations or as cheery color for thank-you cards and announcements.

SPRING
PALETTE OF COLORS

Cotman Watercolors

Permanent Rose   Rose Madder   Lemon Yellow   Sap Green   Cobalt Blue

Designer Gouache

Zinc White

Prismacolor Pencils

Parma Violet   Pink   Yellowed Orange   Canary Yellow

Chartreuse   Aquamarine   Deco Blue   Blue Slate   White

Wedding Invitation

Handmade wedding invitations say something of the thought and care a couple has devoted to planning their wedding. Still, it can be a daunting task to paint a hundred or so invitations by hand. The key is to keep the design simple. Choosing a small image and adding just a brush of watercolor ensures that the project won't become overwhelming. You will streamline production further by using your computer and laser printer to design and print the text.

Finished sizes: Invitation, 4" x 8½";
reception card, 4" x 3½"; reply card, 4¼" x 3½"

Invitation

1. Draft and cut one 4" x 9⅛" rectangle from vanilla card stock. Stamp a flower trio near one 4" edge using gold pigment ink. Sprinkle gold embossing powder on the wet ink, and shake off the excess. Heat with a heating tool to melt the powder. (See "Rubber Stamp Embossing," page 23.)
2. Paint the petals of the flowers rose madder.
3. Using a computer with a laser printer, enter your wedding invitation text in the desired font and size (I used 12-point Edwardian). Center each line, and space the lines to fill a 3" x 6" area, allowing room for the stamped flowers after the last line. Print the text onto the vellum sheet. Trim the vellum to 4" x 8½" so the text is centered. (See "Printing from a Computer," page 24.)
4. Use a bone folder to score the painted card stock panel ⅝" from the top edge. (See step 3 of "Making Standard Cards," page 20.)
5. Fold down on the scored line to make a flap. Tuck the top edge of the printed vellum panel under the flap. Line up the side and bottom edges. Punch two ⅛" holes in the middle of the flap, about ¾" apart, through all layers.
6. Thread the satin ribbon through both holes, front to back, and even up the tails. One at a time, draw each tail to the front through the adjacent hole and pull snug. Trim the tails diagonally.

Materials

Vanilla card stock, two 8½" x 11" sheets
18-lb. Ultra vellum, one 8½" x 11" sheet
⅝"-wide satin ribbon, 6" length
Flower Trio rubber stamp
Gold pigment inkpad
Gold embossing powder
Cotman Rose Madder watercolor
Computer and laser printer
Edwardian computer font (optional)
⅛" hole punch

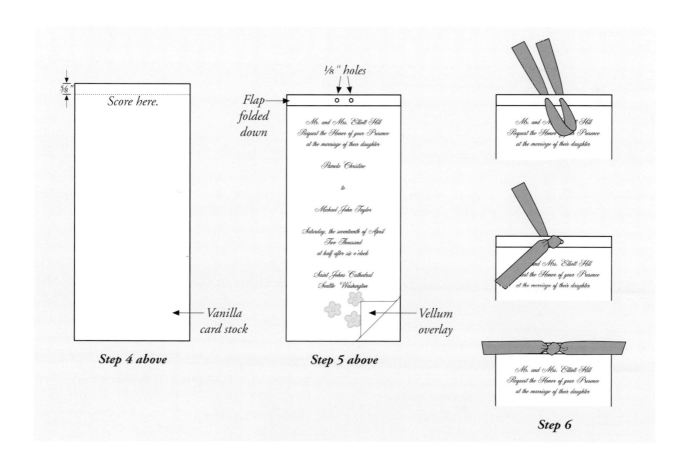

Step 4 above

Step 5 above

Step 6

Tip *Use a smaller inkpad when you want to ink only a portion of a stamp's image.*

Reception and Reply Cards

1. Enter your reception card and reply card texts on the computer, as for the Invitation step 3, referring to the color photo. The text area for each should not exceed 2" x 3". Print both texts onto the remaining vanilla card stock.
2. Stamp one flower trio at the upper left of the reception text and another at the lower right. Sprinkle gold embossing powder on the wet ink, and shake off the excess. Heat with a heating tool to melt the powder.
3. Clean the ink from the flower trio stamp. Ink one flower only and stamp between the upper and lower sections of the reply card text. Emboss with gold powder, as for the reception card.
4. Paint the flower petals rose madder, as for the Invitation, step 2.
5. Cut the card stock to yield one 4" x 3½" reception card and one 4¼" x 3½" reply card.

Tip *Use as little water as possible when painting on card stock. If the card stock begins to buckle or curl, stop painting and let the paper dry completely before adding any more water. Place the painted card stock under a book overnight to flatten it.*

sence

ter

Reception
Immediately Following the Ceremony

Steamboat Inn
Seattle, Washington

Taylor

enth of A

sand

ix o'clock

s C

Was

M _____

_____

Will _____ Attend

avor of a reply is requested
before the 25th of march

Bridal Shower Invitation

This elegant, contemporary format works well for invitations to many types of gatherings, from bridal and baby showers to graduation parties. The leafy border is created by stamping a loose arrangement of leaves, shading them with watercolor, and then cropping the paper edges all around. The design is muted by the soft vellum overlay that contains the invitation's laser-printed text. A blue and purple ombré ribbon carries out the analogous color scheme.

Finished size: 5¼" x 5¼"

Instructions

1. Lightly pencil in a 5⅛" square on the watercolor paper. Using midnight pigment ink, stamp a leaf image onto the paper so that the leaves extend into the square and the stem falls outside it. Repeat to randomly stamp 4 to 6 images around the edge of the square, leaving the middle area free. Sprinkle clear embossing powder on the wet ink, and shake off the excess. Heat with a heating tool to melt the powder. (See "Rubber Stamp Embossing," page 23.)

2. Prewet one leaf interior with water. Put a drop of cobalt blue paint at one end of a leaf, near the stem. The paint will begin moving into the wet area on its own. Meanwhile, rinse the brush and squeeze out the excess water.

3. To create a smooth fade of color, use the brush to pull the color toward the middle of the leaf. Keep the brush on the paper as much as possible.

4. Once you reach the middle of the leaf, see how much paint you have remaining on your brush—is it running out or is it still pretty strong? If it is running out, simply continue slowly across the leaf until the color disappears. If the color is still strong, rinse the brush and squeeze out the excess water before continuing. Your goal is a smooth fade of color across the leaf to the tip. (See "Painting a Watercolor Wash," page 10.)

5. Repeat steps 2–4, prewetting and coloring 3 to 4 leaves at a time. Let dry.

6. Using a computer with a laser printer, enter your invitation text in the desired font and size (I used 12-point French Script). Center each line, and space the lines so the text will not exceed a 3" x 3" area. Print the text onto the vellum sheet. (See "Printing from a Computer," page 24.)

7. Trim the leaf piece to 5" square so the painted leaves run off the newly cut edge. Trim the vellum to 4¾" square. Using double-coated tape, mount the leaf piece on the denim card stock. Center the printed vellum on top. Punch two ¼" holes, about ¾" apart, at the top center through all the layers.

8. Thread the ends of the ombré ribbon through the holes from the back. Tie in a bow on the front.

Step 1

Materials

Denim card stock, 5¼" square
Watercolor paper, about 7" square
29-lb. vellum, one 8½" x 11" sheet
1½"-wide Midori blue ombré wire-edged ribbon, ½ yd.
Leaf rubber stamp
Midnight pigment inkpad
Clear embossing powder
Cotman Cobalt Blue watercolor
Computer and laser printer
French Script computer font (optional)
Double-coated tape
¼" hole punch

 Using a heavier weight vellum, such as 29-lb. or 36-lb., will soften the image underneath.

 Square card formats cost slightly more to mail. Check with your post office for exact charges.

Bouquet Card

This unusual card features a dimensional bouquet. A layer of vellum is riveted to the flowery panel underneath, creating an ethereal, shadowy effect. The illusion is achieved by mounting a few individual blooms on thick foam tape, which raises them up off the surface. The result is like looking through a frosty window pane. Everything about this design is understated and elegant, from the soft blue color scheme to the laser-printed *Congratulations*. A personal message can be written on the back.

Finished size: 5⅞" x 5⅞"

Instructions

1. Using midnight pigment ink, stamp a cluster of 7 flowers, about 3" across, onto the sky blue card stock. Stamp 5 extra flowers along the edge of the card stock (to be cut out and mounted later). Let dry completely (30 to 40 minutes) before coloring.

Step 1

2. Use the white pencil to color all the flower petals. Press hard so the white is opaque and stands out from the sky blue background.

3. Use the blue slate pencil to outline the center of each flower, fading toward the interior. (See "Colored Pencil Fading," page 15.) Color the interior deco blue, and blend into the slate blue outline. (See "Colored Pencil Blending," page 16.)

4. Trim the sky blue card stock to 4⅞" square so the flower cluster is centered. Cut out the 5 extra flowers individually. Affix a small piece of foam tape to the back of each one. Mount them on the cluster to create a dimensional bouquet.

5. Using a computer with a laser printer, enter "Congratulations" in the desired font and size (I used 12-point French Script). Print the text onto the vellum sheet. (See "Printing from a Computer," page 24.)

6. Trim the vellum to 5⅞" square so the text is centered. Center the printed vellum over the bouquet square, so it overhangs by ½" all around. At each corner of the bouquet square, punch a ⅛" hole through both layers and install a light blue eyelet. (See "Installing an Eyelet," page 22.) When all four corners are riveted, the vellum will hug the raised bouquet in the middle of the card.

Step 4

Materials

Sky blue card stock, one 8½" x 11" sheet
29-lb. vellum, one 8½" x 11" sheet
4 light blue ⅛" eyelets
Foam mounting tape
Five-Petal Flower rubber stamp
Midnight pigment inkpad
Prismacolor pencils:
    White
    Deco Blue
    Blue Slate
Computer and laser printer
French Script computer font (optional)

Tip *To gauge the finished effect, lay the vellum on top of the flowers. The only color to show through should be the white petals and the blue flower centers.*

Framed Charm Card

A simple wash of color is all that is needed to highlight this simple stamped frame. The card interior is left white—the perfect spot to mount a charm or other embellishment. When you're planning a wash, choose a stamp-pad ink in a coordinating color. Here, the frame image was stamped in dark navy ink instead of black to coordinate better with the soft blue wash. Relating the colors in this way makes for an unobtrusive background and helps focus attention on the charm in the middle.

Finished size: 4¼" x 5½"

Instructions

1. Stamp a frame onto watercolor paper using midnight pigment ink. Sprinkle clear embossing powder on the wet ink, and shake off the excess. Heat with a heating tool to melt the powder. (See "Rubber Stamp Embossing," page 23.)

2. Prewet the area surrounding the frame with water. Using cobalt blue watercolor, paint a 5" x 5" box around the frame. The blue will begin drifting into the wet area toward the frame.

3. Rinse the brush and squeeze out the excess water. Use the brush to help pull the color towards the frame. If the area surrounding the frame is still fairly wet, the color will become very soft and light. If the area seems dry, rewet it and then pull the color into it, keeping your brush on the paper as much as possible. (See "Painting a Watercolor Wash," page 10.) Let dry.

Step 3

4. Trim the frame piece to 3½" x 3⅝" so the frame is centered. Using double-coated tape, mount the frame piece on the chalk card stock. Mount the card stock on the note card. Use a small piece of foam tape to mount the charm within the frame.

Materials

Handmade Lavender note card, 4¼" x 5½" (folded size)
Chalk card stock, 3⅝" x 3¾"
Watercolor paper, about 5½" x 5½"
Ceramic cake charm
Frame rubber stamp
Midnight pigment inkpad
Clear embossing powder
Cotman Cobalt Blue watercolor
Double-coated tape

Tip *Remember to squeeze the excess water from your brush after rinsing it. If a brush is loaded with water when it touches a painted area, it will push that paint out of the way and create an open spot.*

Butterfly Card

Make this card to send get well wishes or just to say "Happy Spring." The flow of watercolor creates a cheery halo around the butterfly and provides a soft backdrop to the bright "confetti" added at the end. The card is completed in two steps. First, the background wash and butterfly are painted and allowed to dry. Then the brush is loaded with paint, held above the card, and tapped to release a spray of tiny droplets. This easy spatter technique can help camouflage any stray marks you didn't mean to happen!

Finished size: 4¼" x 7¾"

Instructions

1. Stamp a butterfly onto the watercolor paper using midnight pigment ink. Sprinkle clear embossing powder on the wet ink, and shake off the excess. Heat with a heating tool to melt the powder. (See "Rubber Stamp Embossing," page 23.)

2. Prewet the area surrounding the butterfly with plain water. Dilute permanent rose paint with water to create a pale pink color. Paint a 3" x 4" box around the butterfly. The color will drift into the wet area and fade out as it nears the butterfly, for a soft glow.

3. Mix the permanent rose and cobalt blue watercolors with white gouache to make a soft lavender. Paint the butterfly wings. Let dry thoroughly (1 to 2 hours) before moving to step 4.

4. Load your brush with permanent rose paint. To create a spatter effect, hold out your finger over the butterfly and tap the brush handle against it. The vibration will cause paint droplets to flick off the brush bristles onto the paper below. Repeat with cobalt blue and lemon yellow. Let dry.

5. Trim the butterfly piece to 2¼" x 3". Fold the sky blue card stock in half to make a 4¼" x 7¾" card. Open the card and lay it flat. Layer the vellum and the butterfly piece on the card front (see the color photo); the vellum margin should be ¼" on the sides and bottom, but ⅛" at the top. Punch a ⅛" hole at the top center through all three layers and install a pink eyelet. (See "Installing an Eyelet," page 22.)

Materials

Sky blue card stock,
    8½" x 7¾"
18-lb. vellum,
    2¾" x 3⅜"
Watercolor paper, about
    4" x 5"
Pink ⅛" eyelet
Butterfly rubber stamp
Midnight pigment
    inkpad
Clear embossing powder
Cotman watercolors:
    Permanent Rose
    Lemon Yellow
    Cobalt Blue
Designer Gouache Zinc
White

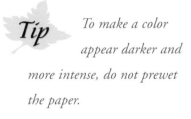

Tip — *To make a color appear darker and more intense, do not prewet the paper.*

Tip — *In a spatter technique, always do the first few taps over scrap paper to eliminate the largest droplets.*

Baby Announcement

Baby announcements should be sweet and simple—sweet in honor of the family's newest little addition, and simple because the new mom and dad will have extra demands on their time and energy. This uncluttered layout calls for just a few touches of watercolor. No blending is involved, but the colors still look lovely under their vellum overlay. Choose a cute or contemporary font, or even write the details on the vellum by hand using a permanent pen. This is a memento your kids will love you for keeping.

We are pleased
to announce the arrival
of

Emma Ruth Hill

born March 9, 2000
weighing 7 lb 4 oz
and measuring 20 in.

Finished size: 5½" x 5½"

Instructions

1. Using midnight pigment ink, stamp the floral border onto water-color paper 4 times to make a "frame" about 5" square. Sprinkle clear embossing powder on the wet ink, and shake off the excess. Heat with a heating tool to melt the powder. (See "Rubber Stamp Embossing," page 23.)
2. Prewet the area inside the frame with water. Dilute permanent rose paint with water to make a medium pink color. Paint the wet area pink, loosely following the curved inside edges.
3. With a No. 6 round brush, paint the leaves green, using a mix of cobalt blue and lemon yellow. Paint the flower petals lavender, using a mix of permanent rose and cobalt blue. Paint the center of each flower cobalt blue. Let dry.

Step 3

4. Using a computer with a laser printer, enter your baby announcement text in the desired font and size (I used 12-point Garamouche). Center each line, and space the lines so the text will not exceed a 3" x 3" area. Print the text onto the vellum sheet. (See "Printing from a Computer," page 24.)
5. Trim the floral border piece to 5½" x 5½" so the frame is centered. Trim the vellum to 5" x 5". Center the printed vellum on the floral border piece so the text appears inside the pink framed area. Punch two ⅛" holes, about ¾" apart, near the top center through both layers. Thread the satin ribbon through both holes, front to back, and even up the tails (as shown for the Wedding Invitation, step 6, page 29). One at a time, draw each tail to the front through the adjacent hole and pull snug. Trim the tails diagonally.

Materials

Watercolor paper, about
    7½" x 7½"
18-lb. vellum, one
    8½" x 11" sheet
⅝"-wide Woad Blue double-
    faced satin ribbon, 6"
    length
Floral Border rubber stamp
Midnight pigment inkpad
Clear embossing powder
Cotman watercolors:
    Permanent Rose
    Lemon Yellow
    Cobalt Blue
Computer and laser printer
Garamouche computer font
    (optional)
⅛" hole punch

Tip *If you have diffi-culty filling large areas with paint quickly and smoothly, try using a 1"-wide flat brush, instead of a No. 4 or No. 6 round brush.*

Baby Carriage Card

O ne way of adding extra depth to your painting is to fill the entire piece of watercolor paper with color. In this card, a purply blue wash helps set off and highlight the pink carriage. This technique is especially effective when you want to make a plain white background appear less stark.

Finished size: 4¼" x 5½"

Instructions

1. Stamp the baby carriage onto watercolor paper using midnight pigment ink. Sprinkle clear embossing powder on the wet ink, and shake off the excess. Heat with a heating tool to melt the powder. (See "Rubber Stamp Embossing," page 23.)
2. Prewet a 3" x 3" area around the carriage. Tint the water slightly, if necessary, to make the wet area easier to see.
3. Mix the permanent rose and cobalt blue watercolors with white gouache to create a soft lavender. Paint the prewetted area, filling it in solidly with color (see the color photo).
4. Dilute permanent rose paint with water to make a soft pink color. Prewet the carriage body, hood, and wheels, and paint them pink.
5. Paint the button at the base of the hood lemon yellow.
6. Trim the baby carriage piece to 3¼" x 3½". Using double-coated tape, mount the baby carriage piece on the rose card stock. Mount the rose card stock on the note card.

Materials

Sky blue note card, 4¼" x 5½" (folded size)
Handmade Rose card stock, 3¾" x 4"
Watercolor paper, about 5" x 5½"
Baby Carriage rubber stamp
Midnight pigment inkpad
Clear embossing powder
Cotman watercolors:
    Permanent Rose
    Lemon Yellow
    Cobalt Blue
Designer Gouache Zinc White
Double-coated tape

Try these alternative color schemes to create an entirely different look.

Emerald, Lemon Yellow, and Permanent Rose

Permanent Rose and Cadmium Yellow

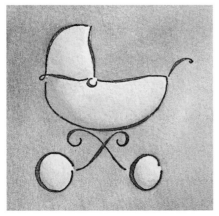

Permanent Rose and Cobalt Blue

Tip *Adding a little white gouache to your watercolor mix makes the paint more opaque and improves the viscosity. Try a gouache mix over a prewetted area when you want smooth, even color coverage.*

Flower Patch Card

This mixed-media project is a spring greeting and all-occasion card rolled into one. The watercolors are applied first, to color the sky, landscape, and stamped house. The colored pencils are used for the fantasy flowers. Color carefully with the pencils so you do not chip off any of the embossed lines.

Finished size: 4¼" x 5½

Instructions

1. Stamp the garden patch onto watercolor paper using black pigment ink. Sprinkle clear embossing powder on the wet ink, and shake off the excess. Heat with a heating tool to melt the powder. (See "Rubber Stamp Embossing," page 23)
2. Mix the sap green and lemon yellow watercolors to make acid yellow. Prewet the area around the house with water, brushing right over the embossed flowers.
3. Starting from the bottom, brush the acid yellow paint around the base of the house and across the path. Slowly work your way up, adding more water to the paint so that the color gradually lightens behind the flower stems. If the paper seems to be drying out, rinse your brush, rewet the paper with plain water, and continue painting. Let dry completely.

Step 3

4. Paint in a hill freehand using sap green. Let dry completely.
5. Mix a bit of permanent rose with the cobalt blue, just enough to add a violet tinge to the blue. Paint the house, concentrating the violet tones at the bottom and the bluer tones toward the top. Paint the window boxes permanent rose.
6. Use the pink and assorted blue pencils to randomly color in the flowers for a cheerful wildflower look.
7. Color the house door and windows canary yellow and yellowed orange. Color the path chartreuse and canary yellow.
8. Trim the flower patch piece to 2⅝" x 3". Using double-coated tape, mount the flower patch piece on the denim card stock. Mount the denim card stock on the note card.

Materials

Handmade Yellow note card, 4¼" x 5½" (folded size)
Denim card stock, 2⅞" x 3¼"
Watercolor paper, about 4½" x 5"
Garden Patch rubber stamp
Black pigment inkpad
Clear embossing powder
Cotman watercolors:
    Sap Green
    Cobalt Blue
    Permanent Rose
    Lemon Yellow
Prismacolor pencils:
    Pink
    Yellowed Orange
    Canary Yellow
    Chartreuse
    Aquamarine
    Deco Blue
    Ultramarine
Double-coated tape

Tip   *Keep your pencil points sharp in order to fill small spots in the design without nicking the embossing.*

Summer

Along with warm, sunny weather, summer brings a huge array of colors. The trees are bursting with a million shades of green. With every sunrise, pinks, reds, and golden tones are washed across the horizon. Clouds are vivid with purples and blues. Summer is a season when colors are bright and pure—nothing can be too blue, too red, or too green. Summer welcomes colors in all their glorious, dramatic intensity.

SUMMER
PALETTE OF COLORS

Cotman Watercolors

| Permanent Rose | Rose Madder | Dioxazine Violet | Cadmium Red Deep Hue | Yellow Ochre |

| Cadmium Yellow Light | Lemon Yellow | Intense Green | Sap Green | Cobalt Blue | Turquoise |

Prismacolor Pencils

| Aquamarine | Light Aqua | Blue Slate | True Blue | Ultramarine |

| Lavender | Imperial Violet | Parma Violet | Mulberry | Magenta | Scarlet Lake |

| Hot Pink | Poppy Red | Orange | Yellowed Orange | Canary Yellow | Chartreuse |

House on a Hill Card

This card uses watercolor blending to achieve a playful lighting effect. Colors are applied at opposite ends of each shape in the stamped image and then pulled together to create a brand-new middle color. A smooth blend is crucial for this dazzling effect and can be achieved by using plenty of paint and keeping the area wet as you fill in. Note how the analogous yellow/green/blue background makes the purple house at the center pop out.

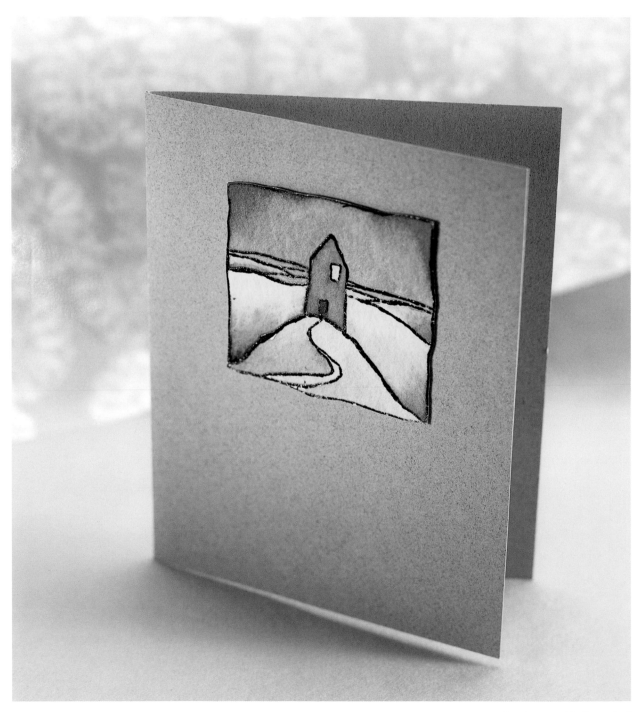

Finished size: 4¼" x 5½"

Instructions

1. Stamp the house on a hill image onto watercolor paper using black pigment ink. Sprinkle clear embossing powder on the wet ink, and shake off the excess. Heat with a heating tool to melt the powder. (See "Rubber Stamp Embossing," page 23.)

2. Squeeze some lemon yellow paint onto a palette. Mix in a drop or two of water—just enough to make the paint spreadable without diluting the color. Paint the two large side hills on each side of the house, starting at the top and stopping about three-quarters of the way down.

3. Paint the remainder of each large side hill using a mix of cobalt blue and sap green. This green mixture will overpower the yellow, so apply it sparingly and don't pull the green into the yellow area too far; just do a little cautious mixing where the yellow and green meet. If you are using enough liquid, the paint will do most of the work for you. (See "Blending Watercolors," page 11.)

Materials

Lavender note card,
   4¼" x 5½" (folded size)
Watercolor paper, about
   4" x 4"
House on a Hill rubber
   stamp
Black pigment inkpad
Clear embossing powder
Cotman watercolors:
   Cobalt Blue
   Turquoise
   Permanent Rose
   Lemon Yellow
   Intense Green
   Sap Green
Double-coated tape

Tip   To avoid spotting and streaking on dry paper, work quickly while the paint is still wet.

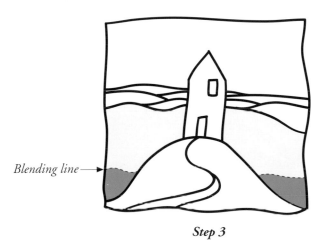

Blending line →

Step 3

4. Paint the remaining distant hills lemon yellow. Add a drop of the green mixture to the bottom or side edge of each outlined area. Let the green and yellow paints run together.

5. Squeeze some cobalt blue paint onto a palette and dilute with water, as in step 2. Paint the upper right and left corners of the sky, drawing the blue color about halfway to the house. Paint the remainder of the sky using a mix of turquoise and intense green, and draw it into the cobalt blue areas.

6. Mix the sap green and lemon yellow watercolors to make chartreuse. Paint the hill in the foreground from left to right, adding more water to the mix as you go to lighten the color.

7. Mix permanent rose and cobalt blue to make purple. Paint the house purple. Paint the door cobalt blue. Paint the window and the path lemon yellow. Let dry.

8. Cut out the scene as close as possible to the embossed outline. Using double-coated tape, mount the cutout on the note card.

Step 5

Swirly Butterfly Card

O nce you have acquired some skill at blending, you are ready to add more depth to your painting. In the previous projects, the colors were all applied directly over a white background. In this exercise, you will see how layering one color over another can add richness and complexity to your image. First, you will paint an underlayer of yellow, then you will paint over it with a blend of blues and greens. The underlayer will show through where the second layer wasn't painted, brightening the entire image.

Finished size: 5¼" x 5¼"

Instructions

1. Stamp the swirly butterfly onto watercolor paper using black pigment ink. Sprinkle clear embossing powder on the wet ink, and shake off the excess. Heat with a heating tool to melt the powder. (See "Rubber Stamp Embossing," page 23.)

2. See "Layering Watercolors," page 12. For the underpainted layer, paint the butterfly wings and the body cadmium yellow. Let dry overnight.

3. Prewet the 4½"-square area surrounding the butterfly with water. Dilute turquoise paint with water to create a pale aqua color. Paint the wet area around the butterfly. Let dry 1 hour.

4. For the top layer, mix the cadmium yellow and intense green watercolors to create a grassy green color. Brush this green color onto a butterfly wing, starting from the body and working out about halfway; as you work, leave some areas open to create a yellow spotted pattern. Rinse the brush and squeeze out the excess water.

5. Apply turquoise paint to the other end of the wing in the same way. Paint toward the green paint until the two colors touch. If the two paints are very wet, simply let them mingle by themselves to create an interesting edge pattern. If they don't mingle on their own, swirl the touching edges slightly with the tip of your brush to help the paints flow together.

6. Repeat steps 4 and 5 for each butterfly wing. Let dry.

7. Trim the butterfly piece to 3½" x 3½". Fold the lavender card stock in half to make a 5¼" x 5¼" card. Open the card and lay it flat. Using double-coated tape, mount the butterfly piece on the denim card stock. Mount the denim card stock on the lavender card. At each corner of the denim square, punch a ⅛" hole and install a baby blue eyelet. (See "Installing an Eyelet," page 22.)

Materials

Lavender card stock,
    10½" x 5¼"
Denim card stock,
    4" x 4"
Watercolor paper, about
    5½" x 5½"
Four ⅛" baby blue eyelets
Swirly Butterfly rubber
    stamp
Black pigment inkpad
Clear embossing powder
Cotman watercolors:
    Cadmium Yellow Light
    Intense Green
    Turquoise
Double-coated tape

Step 4

Step 5

As an alternative, colored pencils allow you to add lots of color with greater control.

Bunny Card

This is a wonderful card to help you learn how to put "suggestive" elements in a painting. The background is a quick splash of blue for the sky and a bit of green for the hill. Those two elements come together to create a whole scene. The beauty of this technique is its speed. The blue is literally laid down with just a few brushstrokes, for the feel of sky peeking through the clouds. Paint the green mound and instantly you have a platform for two bunnies!

Finished size: 4¼" x 5½"

Instructions

1. Using black pigment ink, ink two of the four bunnies on the stamp. Stamp the inked image onto watercolor paper. Sprinkle clear embossing powder on the wet ink, and shake off the excess. Heat with a heating tool to melt the powder. (See "Rubber Stamp Embossing," page 23.)
2. Dilute cobalt blue with water to create a pale blue color. Paint just inside the right edge of the bunny bodies, heads, and ears to suggest shadows.
3. Paint a dot of rose madder onto the bunny noses. Set aside to dry.
4. Lightly pencil in a 3¾" box on the white laid card stock. For the sky, paint a few loose strokes of cobalt blue across the upper two-thirds of the box. Rinse the brush and squeeze out the excess water. For the hillside, paint a green dome shape across the lower third.

Materials

Moonbeam note card, 4¼" x 5½" (folded size)
Aqua card stock, 3½" square
White laid card stock, about 5" square
Watercolor paper, about 3" square
Four Bunnies in a Row rubber stamp
Black pigment inkpad
Clear embossing powder
Cotman watercolors:
    Cobalt Blue
    Rose Madder
    Sap Green
Foam mounting tape
Double-coated tape

Step 5

Step 4

5. When the bunny pair is thoroughly dry, cut it out using an X-Acto knife. Using foam tape, mount the bunnies on the painted card stock, as if they were sitting on the hillside. Trim this scene to 3¼" x 3¼" so the bunnies are centered. Using double-coated tape, mount the bunny scene on the aqua card stock. Mount the aqua card stock on the moonbeam note card.

Birthday Cake Card

Y ou'll use a beginning stamping technique—sponging—to add the soft yellow glow around this birthday cake. The color scheme relies heavily on warm colors—bright reds, oranges, and brilliant chartreuse. Small images like this cake are a good choice for colored pencil work, since the pencil points can reach easily into tight areas. Try blending a few colors into the wisp of flame. Colored pencils make the details easy.

Finished size: 4" x 8½"

Instructions

1. Stamp a birthday cake onto off-white laid card stock using black dye-based ink. Let dry completely (30 to 40 minutes) before coloring.
2. Use the canary yellow pencil to color the top of the cake and the candle flame. Make a small yellowed orange mark in the center of flame, then rub over it with canary yellow.
3. Color the candle orange. Color the dots of frosting on the cake chartreuse.
4. Color the remaining frosting yellowed orange.
5. Color the bottom layer of the cake poppy red, pressing hard near the side edges and using less pressure in the middle. Go over the middle area with orange, rubbing it into the poppy red area; leave a bit of poppy red on the sides untouched.
6. Rub the makeup sponge onto the yellow inkpad to pick up some color. Gently dab the sponge onto the watercolor paper all around the cake. Press lightly and evenly, without twisting, to slowly build up the color. Let dry.
7. Trim the cake piece to 2" x 2". Fold the crimson card stock in half to make a 4" x 8½" card. Using double-coated tape, mount the cake piece on the celery rib card stock, then mount both on the crimson card.

Materials

Crimson card stock, 8" x 8½"
Celery Rib card stock, 2½" x 2½"
Off-white laid card stock, about 4" x 4"
Birthday Cake rubber stamp
Black dye-based inkpad
Yellow dye-based inkpad
Fine-pore makeup sponge
Prismacolor pencils:
    Chartreuse
    Poppy Red
    Orange
    Yellowed Orange
    Canary Yellow
Double-coated tape

Tip   *For a different look, make a fancy border for your cake as shown. The yellows, oranges, and reds work together to create an analogous color scheme.*

Tip   *If an area is extremely small or tight, just fill it in with a solid color.*

Potted Flower Card

This card shows how color intensity can affect a composition. The soft yellow watercolor background, pale red and orange pot, and light green leaves form an understated backdrop for the stronger red flower petals. You can use a contrast between light and dark to make any area you choose more prominent. Simply add a little more water to the areas you wish to lighten. Note how the crimson paper picks up the red flower petals and adds to their intensity.

Finished size: 4¼" x 5½"

Instructions

1. Stamp the flower in pot onto watercolor paper using black pigment ink. Sprinkle clear embossing powder on the wet ink, and shake off the excess. Heat with a heating tool to melt the powder. (See "Rubber Stamp Embossing," page 23.)

2. Prewet the area around the flowerpot with water, deliberately making some areas a little wetter than others. Apply a light wash of yellow ochre. (See "Painting a Watercolor Wash," page 10.) The uneven wetting will produce a textured finish.

3. Brush undiluted cadmium red watercolor onto the tips of the petals. Fill in each petal, mixing in some cadmium yellow right on the paper for a smooth, graduated change. Rinse the brush and squeeze out the excess water. Paint the center of the flower cadmium yellow.

4. Paint the edges of the leaves with a light touch of sap green, then fill in the centers with a bit of yellow ochre.

5. To paint the flowerpot, begin by brushing some slightly diluted cadmium red along the left edge. Fill in the pot, mixing in diluted yellow ochre, cadmium yellow, and more cadmium red as you go. Add a touch of sap green to the red to create a brown shade in the pot interior. Let dry.

6. Trim the flowerpot piece to 2" x 3¼". Using double-coated tape, mount the flowerpot piece on the celery rib card stock, then mount both on the crimson note card.

Materials

Crimson note card,
   4¼" x 5½"
   (folded size)
Celery Rib card stock,
   2½" x 3¾"
Watercolor paper, about
   4" x 5"
Flower in Pot rubber
   stamp
Black pigment inkpad
Clear embossing powder
Cotman watercolors:
   Yellow Ochre
   Cadmium Yellow
      Light
   Sap Green
   Cadmium Red Deep
      Hue
Double-coated tape

Flower Wreath Card

One of the bonuses of rubber stamps is the way they lend themselves to repetition. For this card, one stamp was used to produce six watercolor cutouts. When mounted together in a circle on the card, these rose cutouts form a lovely floral wreath. The overlapping complementary colors really make the design come alive. Other complementary schemes to try with this design are yellow with violet and blue with orange.

Finished size: 4¼" x 5½"

Instructions

1. Stamp six swirl roses (make sure they don't touch one another) onto watercolor paper using black pigment ink. Sprinkle clear embossing powder on the wet ink, and shake off the excess. Heat with a heating tool to melt the powder. (See "Rubber Stamp Embossing," page 23.)

2. Prewet each leaf interior with plain water. For each leaf, put a drop of cadmium yellow light watercolor at the end near the rose. The paint will begin moving into the wet area on its own. Meanwhile, rinse the brush and squeeze out the excess water. Put a drop or two of sap green paint at the other end of the leaf. Slowly move the green toward the yellow, keeping the brush on the surface at all times, to encourage their intermingling. (See "Blending Watercolors," page 11.) Let dry.

3. Paint each rose solidly with cadmium yellow light. Let this underlayer dry overnight.

4. Mix permanent rose and cadmium yellow light to create a warm orange color. Paint around the contours of each rose. Rinse your brush and squeeze out the excess water. Lightly smooth the orange color over the yellow, spreading it thin in some areas so the yellow shines through. Let dry.

5. Cut out the six roses using an X-Acto knife. Affix a small piece of foam tape to the back of each rose. Mount the roses on the saffron card stock, forming a circle about 3¾" in diameter. The roses should overlap the leaves, and the entire wreath should extend a bit beyond the edges of the card stock (see photos).

6. Using double-coated tape, mount the wreath piece on the celery card stock, then mount both on the crimson note card.

Materials

Crimson note card, 4¼" x 5½" (folded size)
Celery card stock, 3½" x 4¼"
Saffron card stock, 3¼" x 4"
Watercolor paper, about 5" x 6"
Swirl Rose rubber stamp
Black pigment inkpad
Clear embossing powder
Cotman watercolors:
  Sap Green
  Permanent Rose
  Cadmium Red
  Cadmium Yellow
    Light
Foam mounting tape

Birthday Presents Card

This card's vivid coloring is due to a combination of complementary colors and blending. The basic idea with blending is to move two colors over one another and then crush them together using the lighter-colored pencil. This produces exciting shading effects and new "in-between" colors. The intensity is increased when complementary colors, such as red and green, are blended side by side, because each one makes the other pop. Note that the pencil colors appear opaque even though the background paper is saffron-colored rather than white.

Finished size: 4¼" x 3"

Instructions

1. Stamp the presents onto saffron card stock using black dye-based ink. Let dry completely (30 to 40 minutes) before coloring.
2. Use the pencils to color the six presents. Work from left to right, coloring one plane surface at a time, as follows.

Step 2

Present 1: Blend Parma violet and lavender.

Present 2: Color the facing surface imperial violet at the top and ultramarine at the bottom, blending them in the middle. Color the polka dots true blue. Color the right side Parma violet. Color the top blue slate.

Present 3: Color the edges of the box lid lightly with chartreuse, then burnish the entire lid with canary yellow. Color the lower left side apple green and chartreuse, blending the colors from left to right. Color the lower right side light aqua and chartreuse, blending from left to right. (See "Colored Pencil Blending," page 16.)

Present 4: Color the stars canary yellow. Blend orange, hot pink, and scarlet lake on the box front, top to bottom. Blend magenta and mulberry, left to right, on the side. Color the top yellowed orange.

Present 5: For the wide green stripes, blend apple green and chartreuse from left to right. For the narrow blue stripes, blend light aqua and aquamarine. Color the top chartreuse. C-76

Present 6: Blend Parma violet and blue slate from left to right. Color the top lavender.

3. Fold the celery rib card stock in half to make a 4¼" x 3" note card. Trim the birthday presents piece to 3¾" x 2½". Using double-coated tape, mount the birthday presents piece on the crimson card stock, then mount both on the front of the note card.

Materials

Celery Rib card stock,
8½" x 3"
Crimson card stock,
4" x 2¾"
Saffron card stock, about
6" x 4½"
Birthday Presents rubber
stamp
Black dye-based inkpad
Prismacolor pencils:
Chartreuse
Aquamarine
Light Aqua
Blue Slate
True Blue
Ultramarine
Lavender
Imperial Violet
Parma Violet
Mulberry
Magenta
Scarlet Lake
Hot Pink
Orange
Yellowed Orange
Canary Yellow
Double-coated tape

Tip — *Changing the direction of your blends can make the image more dynamic. The blending on Present 4 is from top to bottom. The blending on Present 5 is from left to right.*

Five-Petaled Flower Card

The two versions of this design—one bright, the other soft—illustrate how water affects the color intensity. In each version, the same paint colors are used, but the water levels are different. The bright card uses relatively small amounts of water, for strong, intense colors. The softer version uses water more liberally to weaken the colors and achieve pale hints of the original pigment. The cards also differ in their shading. In the bright card the colors appear fairly solid without evidence of fades or washes, but in the soft card there's lots of movement as the colors fade in and out across the surface. By making both cards, you'll get a better feel for the ways water affects the outcome and how to use more or less water in your painting.

Finished size, bright colors: 4¼" x 5½"

Instructions for Bright Colors

1. Stamp a flower onto the watercolor paper using black pigment ink. Sprinkle clear embossing powder on the wet ink, and shake off the excess. Heat with a heating tool to melt the powder. (See "Rubber Stamp Embossing," page 23.)
2. For the background color, mix dioxazine violet and permanent rose watercolors, using as little water as possible. Do not prewet the paper. Beginning at the tip of the right leaf, brush the paint clockwise around the flower image. Work quickly, keeping a wet edge to avoid streaks.
3. Mix a little dioxazine violet into permanent rose to make a deep red color. Paint the petals.
4. Paint the center of the flower and the leaves lemon yellow. Brush sap green along the top edge of the leaves while the yellow is still wet and allow the colors to diffuse into each other. Let dry.
5. Trim the flower piece to 2⅛" x 4¼". Fold the lavender card stock in half to make a 4¼" x 5½" card. Using double-coated tape, mount the flower piece on the royal purple card stock, then mount both on the front of the lavender card.

Painting with less water produces brighter colors.

Materials

Handmade Lavender card stock, 8½" x 5½"
Royal Purple card stock, 2⅜" x 4½"
Watercolor paper, about 4" x 6"
Five-Petal Flower rubber stamp
Black pigment inkpad
Clear embossing powder
Cotman watercolors:
    Permanent Rose
    Dioxazine Violet
    Lemon Yellow
    Sap Green
Double-coated tape

Tip *If you find that the paint dries out faster than you can paint, try a larger round brush or a 1" flat brush. You may be able to fill background areas more evenly with larger brushes.*

Finished size, soft colors: 4¼" x 6¼"

Instructions for Soft Colors

1. Stamp a flower onto the watercolor paper using black pigment ink. Sprinkle clear embossing powder on the wet ink, and shake off the excess. Heat with a heating tool to melt the powder. (See "Rubber Stamp Embossing," page 23.)

2. For the background color, dilute dioxazine violet with plain water to make a pastel shade. Prewet the area surrounding the flower with water. Using the pastel violet watercolor, paint a 3" x 6" box around the flower. The violet paint will drift into the wet areas of the paper toward the flower.

3. Rinse the brush and squeeze out the excess water. Use the brush to help pull the color toward the flower, so that it becomes even softer and more diffused. Continue until the entire background is tinted. (See "Painting a Watercolor Wash," page 10.)

4. Prewet the flower petals. Paint the inside edges of the petals using a mix of permanent rose and dioxazine violet. Pull the color so it fades toward the center of the flower.

5. Dilute the lemon yellow paint with water to make a soft yellow color. Prewet the center of the flower and the leaves, and paint them yellow. Shade the flower center with a watery mix of permanent rose and lemon yellow. Brush diluted sap green along the tops of the leaves. Let dry.

6. Trim the flower piece to 2⅛" x 4½". Fold the rose card stock in half to make a 4¼" x 6¼" card. Using double-coated tape, mount the flower piece on the royal purple card stock, then mount both on the rose card.

Materials

Handmade Rose Card stock, 8½" x 6¼"
Royal Purple card stock, 2⅜" x 4¾"
Watercolor paper, about 4" x 6½"
Five-Petal Flower rubber stamp
Black pigment inkpad
Clear embossing powder
Cotman watercolors:
    Permanent Rose
    Dioxazine Violet
    Lemon Yellow
    Sap Green
Double-coated tape

Painting with more water makes for softer colors.

Autumn

Every year, autumn works its mysterious alchemy, turning the happy colors of summer a little darker and more complex. Brilliant reds fade to rich, deep purple, bright greens turn olive, and earth tones creep up into the trees and fill their branches with ochre, rust, and burgundy leaves. The season of fall offers a new set of colors to work with. This golden palette turns up in the glow of a Halloween pumpkin, a ripening field, and leaves that have fallen to the ground. As if to ward off the cooler weather, autumn offers us colors that are full of warmth.

AUTUMN
PALETTE OF COLORS

Cotman Watercolors

  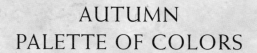

Indian Red   Cadmium Red   Yellow
Deep Hue   Ochre

Prismacolor Pencils

Mulberry   Raspberry   Scarlet Lake   Goldenrod

Burnt   Orange   Yellowed   Canary
Ochre   Orange   Yellow

Deco Yellow   Chartreuse   Limepeel   Olive Green   Apple Green

Teacup Quattro Card

S imple repetition turns a single stamped image into a lively display of dancing teacups. Dark and light colors play off one another here. The red saucers, painted so thickly as to be nearly opaque, are handsomely set off by the surrounding light ochre wash. Note the absence of color inside the teacups, which adds to the drama. By leaving parts of a design blank and allowing the white paper to show through, you add bright highlights to your composition.

Finished size: 5½" x 8½"

Instructions

1. Stamp 4 teacups onto watercolor paper using black pigment ink; arrange the cups in a closely spaced grid, tilting each image slightly so the design is not static. Sprinkle clear embossing powder on the wet ink, and shake off the excess. Heat with a heating tool to melt the powder. (See "Rubber Stamp Embossing," page 23.)

2. Prewet the area around the teacups. Dilute yellow ochre paint with water to make a light wash. Fill in the background, allowing for heavier color saturation in some areas. (See "Painting a Watercolor Wash," page 10.) Let dry.

3. For each saucer, mix Indian red and a little cadmium red, using as little water as possible. Paint the saucer from one end to the other, adding more cadmium red as you go to produce a gradual brightening of the color.

4. For each teacup, mix yellow ochre and a touch of Indian red to make a butterscotch color. Brush this mix along the right edge of the cup. Fill in the area from right to left, adding water to the mix as you go to lighten the color. Leave the inside of the cups white. Let dry.

5. Trim the teacup piece to 4⅜" x 3¾". Fold the vanilla card stock in half to make a 5½" x 8½" card. Using double-coated tape, mount the teacup piece on the nutmeg card stock, then mount both on the vanilla card.

Materials

Vanilla card stock,
   11" x 8½"
Nutmeg card stock,
   4⅝" x 4"
Watercolor paper, about
   6½" x 6"
Teacup rubber stamp
Black pigment inkpad
Clear embossing powder
Cotman watercolors:
   Yellow Ochre
   Indian Red
   Cadmium Red Deep
    Hue
Double-coated tape

Add more water as you approach the left side.

Step 5

Tip: *Drag your brush along the area you want to lighten.*

The brush absorbs excess paint.

Tip   *If the area you just painted appears too solid, you can fix it as long as the paint is still wet. Rinse your brush, squeeze out the excess water, then drag the brush along the side you wish to lighten, as shown at right. The brush will soak up the excess paint, lightening the area. Because the surrounding paint will try to fill the new lightened area, you may have to repeat this procedure several times.*

Cooper's First Sunrise Card

To intensify shades of red and make them appear even more vivid, be sure to include red's complement, green, in your color scheme. Complementary colors are opposite one another on the color wheel. Curiously, they appear dull and brownish when blended or mixed together, but bright and intense when placed side by side. Don't worry if your colors don't correspond to anything in nature—green skies are okay! For textural interest, shade this colored-pencil landscape in two directions: work the hills from the bottom up, to draw attention to the hilltops, and shade the sky in a radial pattern toward the sun.

Finished size: 4¼" x 5½"

Instructions

1. Stamp the sunrise scene onto the sand card stock using black dye-based ink. Let dry completely (30 to 40 minutes) before coloring.
2. Use the pencils to color the sunrise scene. For each hill, start at the bottom and work up, blending raspberry, scarlet lake, orange, and finally yellow. This gives the impression that the light is hitting the tops of the hills. (See "Colored Pencil Blending," page 16.)
3. For the sky, start at the outer edges and work in toward the sun in a radial pattern, blending olive green, limepeel, and chartreuse.
4. Color the sun canary yellow; concentrate the color at the edges and fade toward the center. (See "Colored Pencil Fading," page 15.)
5. Cut out the sunrise scene along the stamped outline. Using double-coated tape, mount the scene inside the card so it is visible through the cutout window. Mount the celery rib window layer to the front of the card, creating a simple matte around the picture.

Materials

Vanilla window card, 4¼" x 5½"
Celery Rib window layer (to fit card)
Sand card stock, about 4" x 4"
Cooper's First Sunrise rubber stamp
Black dye-based inkpad
Prismacolor pencils:
    Chartreuse
    Limepeel
    Olive Green
    Raspberry
    Scarlet Lake
    Orange
    Canary Yellow
Double-coated tape

Change the look of your sunrise by changing the color scheme.

Autumn Tree Card

T his windswept tree has a decided leftward lean, with two leaves actually extending out beyond the picture area. In order to compensate, darker red was added to the right side of the leaves to make them appear heavier, while yellows lighten up the already top-heavy left side. Colored pencils offer control, allowing you to apply many colors in a small amount of space. Here, each leaf is individually colored with three or four shades.

Finished size: 4¼" x 5½"

Instructions

1. Stamp the tree onto the celery smooth card stock using black dye-based ink. Let dry completely (30 to 40 minutes) before coloring.
2. Use the pencils to color the stamped image. For the sky, start at the top corners and sides with canary yellow and fade in toward the middle. Picking up where the canary yellow fades, blend with deco yellow and fade toward the tree. Work lightly around the tree, so the green background shows through. (See "Colored Pencil Fading," page 15, and "Colored Pencil Blending," page 16.)
3. Color the hills top to bottom, blending goldenrod and orange.
4. Color the tree trunk lightly with burnt ochre. Layer deco yellow over it, then shade the right side with mulberry and the lower left side with scarlet lake.
5. Shade each leaf with scarlet lake, orange, and yellowed orange, working from the base to the tip and also from right to left. Then blend the entire leaf with deco yellow.
6. Trim the tree piece to 2⅝" x 4", allowing two leaves to extend beyond the left edge. Using double-coated tape, layer and mount the tree piece, the nutmeg card stock, and the gold metallic card stock on the celery note card.

Materials

Celery Rib note card, 4¼" x 5½" (folded size)
Metallic gold card stock, 3⅜" x 4¾"
Nutmeg card stock, 3⅛" x 4½"
Celery smooth card stock, about 4½" x 6"
Autumn Tree rubber stamp
Black dye-based inkpad
Prismacolor pencils:
    Canary Yellow
    Deco Yellow
    Mulberry
    Scarlet Lake
    Goldenrod
    Burnt Ochre
    Orange
    Yellowed Orange
Double-coated tape

Here's a look at the same autumn tree in two alternate and dramatically different color schemes. In the version at left, the tree is surrounded by a brilliant orange and red wash. The darkened leaves stand out against this glowing background, and the chartreuse hills, with their bright contrast, suggest a blazing sun. The tree done in cool blues and greens gives a far more peaceful feel. The serene background colors make the yellow leaves jump out. The leaves gain extra intensity through touches of orange, which is the complement of the blue-greens used.

Wardrobe Card

This wardrobe image, with its large, open areas, invites colored pencil blending. To add a quirky, antique feel, the red and orange shading on the door panels is done in a random way. The red door panels are set off by a variety of greens, another example of the lively red-and-green complementary color scheme. Large designs like this give you the opportunity to color for an hour or more and really practice and develop your blending skills.

Finished size: 4¼" x 5½"

Instructions

1. Stamp the wardrobe onto the sand card stock using black dye-based ink. Let dry completely (30 to 40 minutes) before coloring.
2. Use the pencils to color the stamped image. For the door panels, work in a general bottom-to-top direction, blending scarlet lake, raspberry, orange, and yellowed orange. Strive to make the color transitions asymmetric and quirky rather than smooth and even. (See "Colored Pencil Blending," page 16.)

Step 2

3. Color the frames around each panel, starting on the inside edge with chartreuse and blending toward the outside edge with limepeel and olive green.
4. Color in the rest of the image with blended areas of chartreuse, limepeel, and olive. Note the bright chartreuse halos around the stars at the top. Color all of the stars yellowed orange. Color the bun feet, blending scarlet lake, raspberry, and mulberry from left to right.
5. Trim the wardrobe piece to 2⅞" x 4⅜". Using double-coated tape, mount the wardrobe piece on the gold metallic card stock, then mount both on the olive note card.

Materials

Handmade Olive note card, 4¼" x 5½" (folded size)
Gold metallic card stock, 3¼" x 4¾"
Sand card stock, about 5" x 6½"
Wardrobe rubber stamp
Black dye-based inkpad
Prismacolor pencils:
    Scarlet Lake
    Orange
    Yellowed Orange
    Chartreuse
    Limepeel
    Olive Green
    Mulberry
    Raspberry
Double-coated tape

Tip To make a color pop out, use its complement nearby. Here, bright orange-red door panels are surrounded by greens.

Pumpkin Card

The background on this pumpkin card offers an exercise in blending three colors over a large area. Plan your blending in advance by figuring out how much of the space you will devote to each color. When applying the pigment, start letting up on the pressure as you approach the area where the next color will start. Following through on these early steps will make the burnishing stage more successful.

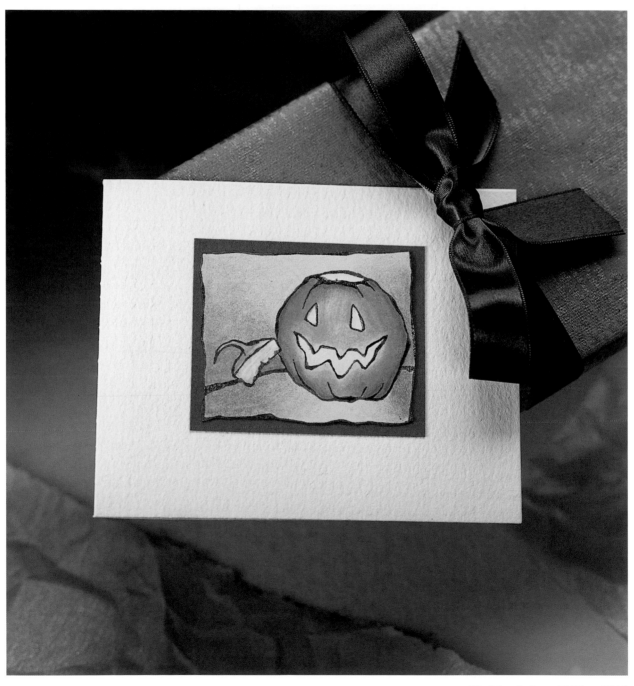

Finished size: 3½" x 2¾"

Instructions

1. Stamp the pumpkin image onto the sand card stock using black dye-based ink. Let dry completely (30 to 40 minutes) before you begin coloring.
2. Use the pencils to color the stamped image. For the sky, start at the base with apple green, then work up, blending in limepeel and then chartreuse. (See "Colored Pencil Blending," page 16.)
3. Color the edges of the foreground limepeel. Blend in chartreuse in the interior to help highlight the pumpkin.
4. Color the edges of the pumpkin orange. Blend in yellowed orange to brighten the face area. Color the eyes, mouth, and top opening deco yellow.
5. Color the top and stem of the pumpkin cap yellowed orange; color the pulp deco yellow.
6. Fold the vanilla card stock in half to make a 3½" x 2¾" note card. Cut out the pumpkin scene along the stamped outline. Using double-coated tape, mount the cutout on the nutmeg card stock, then mount both on the vanilla note card.

Materials

Vanilla card stock,
    7" x 2¾"
Nutmeg card stock,
    2" x 1¾"
Sand card stock, about
    4" x 3½"
Stephanie's Prized
    Pumpkin rubber
    stamp
Black dye-based inkpad
Prismacolor pencils:
    Chartreuse
    Limepeel
    Apple Green
    Orange
    Yellowed Orange
    Deco Yellow
Double-coated tape

Tip   *Use lighter colors in areas where you want to focus attention.*

Step 4

Winter

The year's close brings short days, deep dark nights, and icy landscapes. As if in response, holiday colors brighten the darkness. This juxtaposition results in a considerable color range to enjoy, from a thousand shades of snowy blue and evergreen to brilliant holiday crimsons and golds. Cards for this season offer the perfect opportunity to study the subtle variations in a winter twilight sky, a snowy field, and a perfectly decorated tree.

WINTER
PALETTE OF COLORS

Cotman Watercolors

| Cadmium Red Deep Hue | Cadmium Red Light | Cadmium Yellow | Lemon Yellow |

| Sap Green | Cobalt Blue | Permanent Rose | Indian Red |

Prismacolor Pencils

Scarlet Lake   Process Red   Orange

Canary Yellow   Deco Yellow   Chartreuse   Apple Green

Aquamarine   Blue Slate   True Blue   Copenhagen Blue   White

Christmas Tree Card

This project combines colored pencil and watercolor in two easy applications. Dots of color are worked into the tree with colored pencils, and then paint is filled in around them. Since there's no waiting for the colored pencil dots to dry, as in watercolors, the painting part of the project can begin immediately. The painting can also be fairly loose, since the pencil colors won't run if they get wet.

Finished size: 4¼" x 5½"

Instructions

1. Stamp the Christmas tree onto the watercolor paper using black pigment ink. Sprinkle clear embossing powder on the wet ink, and shake off the excess. Heat with a heating tool to melt the powder. (See "Rubber Stamp Embossing," page 23.)
2. Prewet the area around the tree with plain water. Paint this area cadmium red. Paint a 3" x 4" box around the entire image using Indian red. Allow the two reds to mix by themselves. (See "Painting a Watercolor Wash," page 10.) Let dry.
3. Use the pencils to burnish in small random dots of color on the tree, for Christmas tree lights.
4. Paint the tree sap green, going around the colored lights. Use only a small amount of water, working quickly to maintain a wet edge until the tree is completely filled in. Let dry.
5. Trim the Christmas tree piece to 2⅜" x 3½". Using double-coated tape, mount the Christmas tree piece on the metallic gold card stock, then mount both on the crimson note card.

Materials

Crimson note card, 4¼" x 5½" (folded size)
Gold metallic card stock, 2⅝" x 3¾"
Watercolor paper, about 4½" x 5½"
Christmas Tree rubber stamp
Black pigment inkpad
Clear embossing powder
Cotman watercolors:
  Cadmium Red Deep Hue
  Sap Green
  Indian Red
Prismacolor pencils:
  Aquamarine
  Scarlet Lake
  Orange
  Canary Yellow
Double-coated tape

Painted with a cobalt blue background, then punched with a ¹/₁₆" holepunch to create "snow."

Painted with a cadmium red background, then sprinkled with salt while still wet to create a crackle effect.

Christmas Present Card

This red package gets its golden yellow halo from wet-on-wet blending, a technique that creates very fluid color changes. The paper is prewetted twice, first with plain water and then with yellow watercolor. Green watercolor is then pulled into the yellow area. The result is a smooth halo of color around the central image.

Finished size: 5½" x 4¼"

Instructions

1. Stamp a present onto the watercolor paper using gold pigment ink. Sprinkle gold embossing powder on the wet ink, and shake off the excess. Heat with a heating tool to melt the powder. (See "Rubber Stamp Embossing," page 23.)

2. Prewet the area around the present with plain water. Working quickly, while the paper is still very wet, brush lemon yellow paint around the package, working out about 1" in all directions. (See "Painting a Watercolor Wash," page 10.) Do not rinse the brush.

3. Make sure the paper is still damp, and rewet if necessary. Paint the corners of the paper sap green. Pull the green partway into the yellow, stopping about ¼" from the present so a yellow halo remains around it. (See photo below and "Blending Water-colors," page 11.)

Step 3

4. Paint the left plane surface of the present Indian red. Paint the front cadmium red. Paint the top a mix of Indian red and cadmium red. Let dry.

5. Trim the Christmas present piece to 4¼" x 2½". Fold the crimson card stock in half to make a 5½" x 4¼" note card. Using double-coated tape, mount the Christmas present piece on the gold metallic card stock, then mount both on the crimson note card.

Materials

Crimson card stock, 11" x 4¼"
Gold metallic card stock, 4¾" x 3"
Watercolor paper, about 6½" x 5"
Present rubber stamp
Gold embossing powder
Gold pigment inkpad
Cotman watercolors:
    Lemon Yellow
    Sap Green
    Indian Red
    Cadmium Red Deep
      Hue
Double-coated tape

Snowman Gift Tag

The challenge posed by this stamped image is the irregular background area to be painted. Remember to mix enough paint to carry you through, start to finish. Begin at the left of the snowman and work your way up and around to the lower right, keeping your brush on the paper as much as possible. As you become more comfortable filling in large areas, you'll be able to skip prewetting the paper in order to keep the colors more intense. Uncomplicated images like this one are ideal for gift tags and other projects made in multiples since they can be colored in so quickly.

Finished size: 4½" x 4½"

Instructions

1. Stamp the snowman on the watercolor paper using black permanent ink.
2. Dilute cobalt blue paint with a little water to make a medium blue. Paint the background around the snowman's head, adding a touch of permanent rose now and then to produce purple highlights.
3. Mix the cadmium red and cadmium yellow watercolors to make orange. Paint the carrot nose and hatband.
4. Paint the hat and scarf cadmium red. Let dry.
5. Cut out the snowman picture along the stamped outline. Using double-coated tape, mount the cutout on the silver card stock, then mount both on the indigo card stock. Punch a hole in the upper left corner, and thread with a narrow cord or ribbon.

Why not make a variety of snowman gift tags? The sledding fellow shown here would be a charmer. Carefully fill the background sky with cobalt blue, using plenty of paint for even coverage.

Materials

Indigo card stock,
    4½" x 4½"
Silver metallic card stock,
    3½" x 3½"
Watercolor paper,
    about 5" x 5"
⅛" metallic cord
Snowman rubber stamp
Black permanent ink
Cotman watercolors:
    Cadmium Red Deep
      Hue
    Cadmium Yellow
    Cobalt Blue
    Permanent Rose
Double-coated tape
⅛" hole punch

Tip   *Stamping with permanent ink saves you the step of embossing when you plan to follow up with watercolors. There are many waterproof inks on the market that you can paint over. Some require heat setting and some don't.*

Star Over Neighborhood Card

Once you've mastered simple blending techniques, you'll be ready to tackle this complex blended background—it features almost a dozen different colors. By blending and layering multiple colors, you can make even the most simple composition quite dramatic. A touch of red over a blue background, for example, adds a subtle violet tinge. As you become more comfortable with layering, try unexpected color combinations—oranges on blues, chartreuse on lemon yellow, aquamarine on imperial violets, and so forth.

For this project, you will be coloring on mat board, another excellent coloring surface. Find a board with some tooth, and don't be afraid to really press hard when burnishing. The board's extra thickness will provide the necessary give and add dimension to your card as well.

Finished size: 4" x 4"

Instructions

1. Stamp the image onto mat board using black dye-based ink. Let dry completely (30 to 40 minutes) before coloring.
2. Use the pencils to color the scene. First, blend Copenhagen blue and blue slate, starting at the skyline and working up. (See "Colored Pencil Blending," page 16.)
3. Blend apple green and aquamarine across the top of the sky, from left to right, leaving the area around the star uncolored. Color the star white.
4. Blend in chartreuse and yellow across the same sky area, left to right, to brighten and intensify the blue underlayer. Note the bright yellow aura that develops around the star.
5. Color the extreme foreground, blending Copenhagen blue, blue slate, and aquamarine from left to right.
6. Color the middle ground, blending chartreuse, apple green, Copenhagen blue, and blue slate from left to right.
7. Color the first building on the left deco yellow, working in some scarlet to define the roof line and side walls. Making this building yellow will help counterbalance the bright star and halo on the right side of the picture.
8. Color the remaining buildings by blending deco yellow, orange, scarlet lake, and process red in various combinations. Shift the direction of the blends (horizontal, vertical, diagonal) for each building to add texture.
9. Color the windows aquamarine or Copenhagen blue, pressing firmly for rich, solid color. Color the doors deco yellow, process red, or aquamarine—whichever offers the most contrast.
10. Fold the indigo card stock in half to make a 4" x 4" note card. Using an X-Acto knife, cut out the skyline scene along the stamped outline. Place the cutout scene on the blue denim card stock and trim the card stock ¼" larger all around (the shape will be irregular). Using double-coated tape, mount the scene on the denim card stock, then mount both on the indigo note card.

Materials

Indigo card stock, 8" x 4"
Denim card stock, about 3" x 3"
Mat board, about 4" x 4"
Star Over Neighborhood rubber stamp
Black dye-based inkpad
Prismacolor pencils:
  White
  Deco Yellow
  Chartreuse
  Apple Green
  Aquamarine
  Blue Slate
  True Blue
  Copenhagen Blue
  Scarlet Lake
  Process Red
  Orange
Double-coated tape

Tip

This scene is an example of a warm/cool color scheme. The warm colors such as red and orange seem to pop off the page, while the cool colors such as blue tend to recede.

Step 3

Step 4

Four Snowmen and Star Card

When watercolors are still wet on the paper, they can be manipulated in various ways. If a color is too strong, a dry brush can soak up the excess. If two different colors meet, they will naturally intermingle to create interesting edge patterns. One characteristic behavior is that plain water, when added to wet color, will push the standing pigment out of the way. In this card, letting a single drop of water fall on the star pushes away the blue background color and creates a white halo. Results with this technique are difficult to control—they are a factor of the paper surface, the amount of water, and so forth—but you can experiment. Just remember to add the water while the paint is still wet.

Finished size: 5½" x 4¼"

Instructions

1. Stamp the snowmen onto watercolor paper using black pigment ink. Sprinkle clear embossing powder on the wet ink, and shake off the excess. Heat with a heating tool to melt the powder. (See "Rubber Stamp Embossing," page 23.)

2. Prewet the sky area behind the snowmen. Using cobalt blue watercolor, paint across the wet area from corner to corner, right up to the star outline. Add a touch of permanent rose here and there and mix it in to create purple tones.

3. While the background is still wet, rinse your brush. Let a single drop of clear water fall on the star. The water will push the blue paint away from the star, creating a bright halo. The size of the halo will depend on the amount of water used.

4. Paint the scarves and hats cadmium red, cadmium yellow, sap green, orange (cadmium red plus cadmium yellow), and light green (sap green plus cadmium yellow).

5. Paint the star cadmium yellow. Let dry.

6. Cut out the snowmen on the embossed outline. Using double-coated tape, mount the snowmen on the navy note card.

Step 2

Step 3

Materials

Navy note card,
  5½" x 4¼" (folded size)
Watercolor paper, about
  5½" x 4"
Four Snowmen and Star rubber stamp
Black pigment inkpad
Clear embossing powder
Cotman watercolors:
  Cadmium Red Deep Hue
  Lemon Yellow
  Sap Green
  Cobalt Blue
  Permanent Rose
Double-coated tape

Tip   *Embossed images are extra easy to paint with watercolors. The raised lines keep the wet areas from bleeding into each other.*

Snowman and Star Card

Shadows are easy to paint and add a touch of realism to your work. You'll need to consider light and perspective, two concepts that, while familiar, are probably not foremost in your mind when you're coloring simple rubber-stamped images. In this scene, visualize the star at the upper left corner casting shadows that fall toward the lower right. The shadows don't have to be realistically shaped—a simple blob of color will convey the idea. What makes shadows even easier is that you can use the paint left over on your brush from when you finish painting another area. Your shadow color will be automatically coordinated to the colors in the design and the color will be soft because only a small amount of paint is left on the brush.

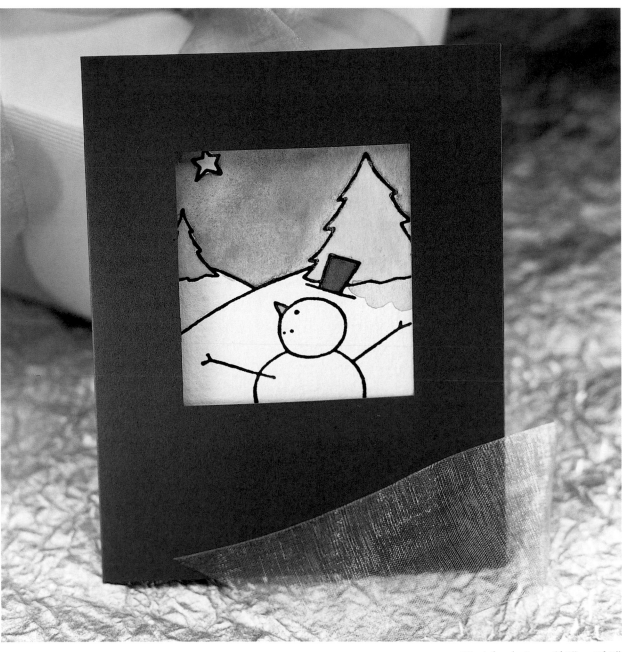

Finished size: 4¼" x 5½"

Instructions

1. Stamp the snowman scene onto the watercolor paper using permanent black ink.
2. Prewet the sky area. Mix cobalt blue and permanent rose to create a purple color. Paint this purple mix across the lower half of the sky. Rinse the brush, but leave it somewhat watery. Next, apply cobalt blue watercolor across the top of the sky. Use the brush to pull the cobalt blue down into the purple area for a gradual mingling of the colors. (See "Blending Watercolors," page 11.)
3. To paint shadows, dilute some cobalt blue paint with water. Brush some of this weak mix to the lower right of both the snowman and the tree on the right, to suggest starlight streaming down from the upper left.
4. Paint the trees pale green, using a diluted mix of sap green and cadmium yellow. Paint the hat red, using a mix of cadmium red and Indian red. Paint the star cadmium yellow. Let dry.
5. Trim the image to 3" x 3½". Using double-coated tape, mount the image inside the card so it is visible through the cutout window.

Materials

Navy window note card, 4¼" x 5½" (folded size)
Watercolor paper, about 5" x 5½"
Snowman and Star rubber stamp
Black permanent ink
Cotman watercolors:
    Sap green
    Cobalt Blue
    Permanent Rose
    Indian Red
    Cadmium Red Deep Hue
    Cadmium Yellow
    Lemon Yellow
Double-coated tape

Tip *Shadow shapes need not be exact. Usually, an appropriately placed "blob" will do, as shown below.*

Single Snowman Card

This card shows you how easy it is to create an entire landscape around a single stamped image. The snowman by himself looks good, but when he's sitting on a snowy hillside with a fabulous evening sky as a backdrop, he's absolutely wonderful. All you do is paint in the sky and the white hillside emerges from the negative space. Just a few short strokes of the watercolor brush and it's finished!

Finished size: 5½" x 8½"

Instructions

1. Stamp the snowman in the center of the watercolor paper using black pigment ink. Sprinkle clear embossing powder on the wet ink, and shake off the excess. Heat with a heating tool to melt the powder. (See "Rubber Stamp Embossing," page 23.)
2. Lightly pencil in a 3¼" x 4¼" rectangle around the embossed snowman. Prewet the sky area, leaving a ½" margin around the side and top edges and curving the lower edge for the hillside. Tint the water slightly, if necessary, to make the wet area easier to see.
3. Mix cobalt blue and permanent rose paint to create a purple color. Paint the sky from the lower left corner, up and over the snowman, down to the lower right; alternate between the cobalt blue paint and the purple mix as you go, intermingling the colors slightly.
4. Paint the carrot nose cadmium red light. Let dry.
5. Fold the twilight card stock in half to make a 5½" x 8½" card. Using double-coated tape, mount the snowman scene on the silver metallic card stock, then mount both on the front of the card.

Materials

Twilight card stock, 11" x 8½"
Silver metallic card stock, 3⅜" x 4⅜"
Watercolor paper, about 5" x 6"
Single Snowman rubber stamp
Black pigment inkpad
Clear embossing powder
Cotman watercolors:
    Cobalt Blue
    Permanent Rose
    Cadmium Red Light
Double-coated tape

Step 3: Start painting at the lower left . . .   *. . . and finish at the lower right.*

Source Guide

Memory Box
(888) 723 1484
e-mail: memoryboxco@home.com
Wholesale inquiries only: 8½" x 11" fine card stock, notecards, window cards, and window layers

Impress Rubber Stamps
(206) 901 9101
www.impressrubberstamps.com
Rubber stamps, art supplies, eyelets and eyelet kits, ribbons, and packaging

Rubbermoon Stamp Company
12670 Strahorn Rd.
Hayden Lake, ID 83835
(208) 772 9772
www. rubbermoon.com
Over 400 artistic rubber stamp designs available ranging from whimsical to contemporary

About the Author

Dave Brethauer works for Impress Rubber Stamps, the largest rubber-stamp retailer and wholesaler in the Northwest. He is one of the designers for the legendary Rubbermoon Stamp Company and owns the Memory Box stationery company with his wife, Monica. He has taught hundreds of students how to incorporate watercolor and colored pencil techniques into their stamping to create beautiful, one-of-a-kind greeting cards.